RATTLED AWAKE VOLUME 11:

The Mental Health Issue

Anthology Authors

Lonnee Rey

CONTENTS

FOREWORD

by Eileen Bild

Life can be an incredible journey filled with triumphs, hope, joy, happiness and love; while also intertwined with challenges, struggles and disempowerment. We are all having a human experience. The question becomes, how well are you navigating the ups and downs?

In this book you will discover the amazing strength that dwells within each of us and when faced with some of life's most impossible curve balls; a will that overpowers everything else. Each story is a testament to every author's tenacity to overcome and then take their knowledge gained to bring this part of themselves into the world as a catalyst for others.

When there is a mass consciousness embroiled in chaos, it can trickle down into the microcosm of the individual experience. The mind is very powerful, giving us the opportunity to collaborate with the universal principles to bring our awareness to higher levels. Lonnee Rey has contributed to making this world a better place through her series of books where she has given a platform for contributing authors to be vulnerable in a raw and heartfelt way.

My own life journey has had its share of boulders dropped on my path with such force that I had no choice but to face it, destroy it and come out the other side empowered. Much of my success comes from practicing techniques and strategies for strong mental and emotional health. Without this training, I am not sure I would be who I am and how far I have come today.

If you want to be inspired and encouraged to be in this world, living your best life with a toolbox filled with valuable life tools, then you will want to read the stories in this book and the others in the series!

We are never alone in this world, and book anthologies like this one are a blessing for both the authors and the readers. When we share our most intimate trials and tribulations, through the process of writing, we relive our experience. This can be daunting and yet liberating. You, the reader, can walk with the authors as they share their hardships, cry and laugh with them, hold their hand in your mind's eye and wish them well in your heart.

All the contributions to this book are based on a mental health crisis, whether from tragedy, dis-ease in the body, choices made gone sideways, or other life altering events. In my case, I had a health crisis that nearly took my life where I had hit rock bottom with "up" the only way out. A declaration set the stage for the next steps that catapulted me into a completely new and extraordinary life.

Lonnee Rey bridges the world of what is with the world of what can be by uniting the stories in this book for the purpose of change. Nothing happens until we do something different and then support this shift with thinking and actions for a solid foundation. The mental world within each of us can be the difference between staying stuck in a repeated pattern or breaking free into an empowering breakthrough from which you will never go back, only forward.

If you have ever desired to go "there" from "here," creating a better life, better version of yourself and finding the treasures that lie within you, then this book is a must read!

*"Fear is only a mask in front of
something greater to step into"*

Eileen Bild

INTRODUCTION

These are not all sad stories - oh no, far from it! Within these pages, tough topics are spoken of with refreshing candor, and solutions offered that may surprise you.

We came together to create a diverse book with one objective in mind: mental health and well-being. Each writer brings a new perspective, from 15 year old Brady finding his tribe at Nerdcore, to "The Mighty One," a hard rock band whose song about suicide, "Kickin' Stones," has become their latest album's top track, to the senior citizens whose lives have suddenly taken a turn for the better.

The honesty, transparency and vulnerability of their stories, along with their passion to reach you, move you, and yes, HELP you, are evident in every heartfelt story.

They are pillars of hope, proving one's future does not have to equal the past. In fact, it can become a dream-come-true.

Thank you for being part of the change we all seek.

GREG SPILLER ... MAKE IT TO THE SHORE

I was alone with my thoughts again. I locked eyes on the chef's knife laying on the counter. It is said that suicidal people don't actually want to die, moreso they don't want to continue living with the life they currently have. This was true for me, although I no longer saw the point in staying alive. As I stared at that 12 inch blade with confliction, I became drenched in fright as the intrusive thoughts now washing over me were no longer hypothetical. What angle do I need to get past my ribs? How hard do I need to thrust to get to my heart on the first try? What would the steel actually feel like as it sinks into my chest? How much blood will there be? I had two choices: pick up the knife, or pick up the phone. I picked up both, not knowing what I was going to do next.

I had become a recluse. I was barely able to bathe and dress myself for work. I should never have been driving, but somehow I made it to work and back each day without killing myself or someone else while behind the wheel. The sluggish drudgery of gridlocked commute played a divine hand as if my mind was on autopilot. I felt like I was.

I wasn't sleeping; rather I would watch the clock tick behind the weight of my dried out eyelids. The lack of sleep had created its own set of problems that spilled into my work. I was desperately holding on by a thread to make eight hours go by as quickly as possible. Every minute of every hour was a blur. Ruminating thoughts darting obsessively back and forth through my mind, further constructing the tower of anxiety I had built that was in constant, critical danger of collapsing in on me.

The tension and torment of what my life had become after divorce reached its pinnacle during dinner celebrating my son's high school graduation. My depression was palpable; the mask was long gone, abandoned with the pretense that things were going to be ok. No one wanted to be around me, as if I was actually capable of sucking their life force with the gravity of my despair. When I look back at the soulless void I was abandoned to, I felt completely and totally lost. Mentally and emotionally discarded to the darkest chasm depleted of any fractal of light. Nothing to orient myself, to even begin trying to find a way out. I had drifted so far into depression I had reached the Absolute Kelvin of hopelessness: the infinite cold, where all atomic motion stops in total absence of warmth or signs of life.

I finally accepted that I needed help with my problems. I couldn't ignore them any longer, or continue putting off dealing with them. The weight of the world, my world, had finally crushed me. I was frozen - mentally, emotionally, spiritually, physically. Still holding the knife inwards towards my chest, there must have been a reason both hands weren't on the knife. I had searched for any information on how to actually kill myself, but wasn't finding the answers I sought. No one wants to be liable for aiding in your death, so there isn't much out there that's easily available. This website actually convinced me NOT to end my life: https://lostallhope.com/ - specifically, the sections asking to consider (and describe) the amount of pain different methods actually cause before you finally die, the (extremely low) probability of success, and how much worse it could be if not successful.

I dialed the phone and made a call for help.

A woman picked up, "....what is your emergency?" "I need help. I need someone to come and get me." Immediately she asked "What kind of help?" "Take this knife away from me and take me to the hospital." I gave my address and collapsed into the couch. Everything I had suppressed spontaneously released like a flood gate and I was drowned in uncertainty. I had finally let go of everything I was so desperately holding onto to have some semblance of control over the life that had diffused into nothingness. Help was finally on its way.

My call for help turned into spending 10 days in the nuthouse. Being held in the psych ward was a whole new nightmare to process. Actual crazy people are truly dangerous, and began targeting me at my most vulnerable. I had never been that on edge with fight-or-flight fear for my life more than the nights spent inside the hospital, terrified my schizophrenic roommate was going to somehow kill me in my sleep, because he told me he would. My entire inpatient stay was an extended hellscape that was of no solace or aid. It was a stark awakening to the glaring shortcomings of mental health services. A callous turnstile where you are sedated as best as possible then quickly tossed out to go be someone else's problem.

My outpatient group therapy was where I began to acknowledge the existence of reality again. My second to last session is where I finally spoke for the first time, only saying my name. The last session I was able to share that I had a debilitating and infinite sadness within me, consuming me. Major Depressive Disorder, and Complex PTSD.

Transitioning from group to individual therapy, I was being forced to return to work, against doctor's recommendations. The week before my return, a glitch in payroll missed a deposit to my bank and launched a shit storm that could not be undone. I was barely hanging on by a thread as it was, going through a divorce and paying for two households, neither of which I could afford. Holding my employer responsible for the financial hardship that it caused, I was fired when my frustration boiled over and was unleashed onto the world. What little money I had quickly ran out, and I was evicted from my apartment. The terror of homelessness was a new reality I was not ready for, and amplified the reasons not to stay in it. You learn quickly and coldly that people will shit on you, especially while you're down, and no matter what you do it's never good enough. I had found the place where single white males are the last and least cared about: social services and housing shelters.

What could possibly be worse than homelessness??? My ex-wife's brother stayed in touch with me throughout and after the divorce. I had known him since he was 11, and I was the older brother he never had. I had been a better sibling to him than his own flesh and blood. We were brothers in bond, and for life. He offered for me to live with him, where I could try to begin picking up the pieces of my shattered life. Little did I know that the house was riddled with its own mental and emotional problems on top of my own, cursed in a town besmirched by the absolute worst far right idealogues hell bent on aggressing everything and everyone damned to live there. No one seemingly understood what I had been through, what I was going through now, or even gave a shit about any of it.

None of this was good for my depression, CPTSD, or my career prospects. Then COVID happened and the entire country virtually stopped. I was forced to survive on pandemic assistance for 3 years, unable to meet any obligations to anyone, not even myself. I was once again viewed in contempt, as a dead beat and a low life for having the unmitigated gall to suffer from major depression and CPTSD. Having almost nothing. Being less than nothing. A suitcase full of clothes, a small box of memories, and identifying documents were all I had left as my only possessions. Still, I had to keep trying to take steps forward; there were conditions for assistance and they were required whether I had depression or CPTSD.

Suddenly, my unemployment benefits and insurance ran out. I was forced to go cold turkey off psych meds, which was another rollercoaster of disorientation and purgatory. In a surprise twist of fate, that experience enveloped into the chef's kiss of vision quests. My mind took a journey back to the beginning of my life, as if I was outside of my own body. I examined many moments of my life that influenced, shaped, and defined who I had become, with illumination as to why. Everything in my life came to make total sense. Over a period of nine days this drug induced psychosis had turned into enlightenment. I now understood why I was the way I was. Self actualization Greg incarnate.

Attempting to rebuild a new life, I was able to get a therapist and medication while on assistance. The best recommendation in town was surprisingly not a terrible person unlike the rest of the locals. I finally had someone who would listen, and not judge my circumstances as my only identity. Just as my previous two couple's counselors had validated, my asks to my ex-wife were reasonable and responsible. My ex-wife had avoided accountability or responsibility, and the pressure of having to overcompensate for it bubbled up into a volcano of grip stress that finally erupted.

I wasn't a terrible person, I was only dealing with terrible people in a terrible situation and taking all the blame for it. It had finally destroyed me.

Through sessions with my new therapist I learned many

things about divorce. The odds were against me in becoming another statistic: 62% of male suicides are unmarried/divorced men - two out of every three; and NINE times more than divorced women. Typically, there are no friends to offer solace or support. Children become distant strangers - parental alienation is real, and the pain from it is unimaginable. Forget about dating. Dating after 35 is like looking for the least damaged item at the thrift store. Being able to trust a woman again to be in a relationship seemed impossible.

Brain fog is another terrifying symptom of depression that affects cognitive functions like working memory, decision making, and the ability to focus. It also makes it difficult to remember things or think through problems. It makes things difficult to work efficiently, socialize, or even complete basic tasks. This amplifies feelings of failure, shame, and hopelessness that creates a vicious cycle with no apparent exit. The existential nihilism of depressive brain fog is that everything you learned is gone; only nothingness exists. Is it gone forever? Twenty years of professional training and experience evaporated from my memory. I didn't think I would ever be able to work in the field of IT again.

Craving a richer understanding, I dove deep into behavioral psychology, depression, CPTSD, and economic stress. Through this path I arrived at discovering the Sigma INFJ. I had also learned about Empaths and people pleasing, and that I was one. Most likely a Highly Sensitive Person to physical and emotional stimulus. I learned more about Narcissists, and that I had been surrounded by them; diving into this further it was determined I was being manipulated by four narcs at the same time, all within my immediate circle. These were the people that were supposed to care about me the most. Breadcrumbs, love bombs, and gaslights oh my! It was time to walk away from narcs and people pleasing, so I cut them from my life. I would no longer serve others at the expense of myself.

The a-ha moment came from the Myers-Briggs personality types; I am identified as INFJ. INFJs are guided by personal values and a need for a meaningful life marked by deep connections. Extremely motivated and persistent in taking positive action, they are problem solvers that believe a job worth doing is worth doing at 110%. They are committed to providing the best quality work, and that the best quality is defined by them, not others. Learning about this reverberated to my core; for the first time in my life I felt totally seen and understood, even to myself.

I was fascinated, and dove even further into personality types. I then came to learn about Sigmas and identified with that as well. Sigmas focus on self-mastery. Known for independence, ability to think critically and strategically, they value their freedom and create their own path instead of conforming to societal expectations.

Continuing my inner work, I developed my own three steps of boundary setting to protect myself and deal with aggressors:

❖ Step 1: calling out the thing that they did, and letting them know - don't do that. Don't go there.

- ❖   Step 2: the 2nd call out, letting them know that I know they know they heard me - seriously, don't do that. Don't go there.

- ❖   Step 3: the entire world stops; they wanted my attention so badly, well now they have it. ALL OF IT. Nothing else exists now except the confrontation with them and how they absolutely will not be doing that, and that there are serious, irreversible consequences if they insist on continuing to do so. Nice Greg goes away, and not-nice Greg steps in his place. Nobody likes that guy. Not nice Greg doesn't match disrespect, he dwarfs it. DO NOT FUCKING TRY HIM. I GUARANTEE YOU WILL NOT LIKE THE OUTCOME.

Armed with this new understanding of self, I set out to rebuild my own life to my own degree.

When you get knocked down repeatedly, you keep asking yourself why would anyone want to stick around for this to keep happening again and again and again......Every time I got knocked to the ground made it that much harder to get back up again. Each time I laid there longer than before. Inert. Inadequate. Indifferent. After the umpteenth time of having the rug pulled out from under me, after just barely getting back on my feet from the last time, barely being able to stand with my fists against the world, a paralyzing dread kicked in. For the first time, I wondered "What's going to be any different this time if I get up again? I'm just going to end up right back here again. Why bother to keep going?"

I had to find a reason to get back up one more time, because getting knocked down over and over was making me not want to anymore.

A voice spoke to me inside my head. I suddenly remembered something I had heard in a viral video short "If you're going through Hell, why would you stay in Hell?" I did not want to stay at rock bottom, that's for damn sure. It had become all too familiar; the repeating body blows of life working me over yet again. A second voice spoke. It was a monologue from a movie "Life will beat you down and keep you there if you let it. It's not how hard you can hit, it's how hard you can get hit and keep moving forward."

My thoughts centered on my sons. What lesson would I be teaching them by giving up and checking out? Is that the legacy I want to leave behind? The final memory of me? Little did I know then, but there was something different about the next time I got up. The answer was ME. I was different this time. I was resolved to show my kids that giving up is never the answer to life's problems. Perseverance becomes strengthened. Endurance turns forged. Grit is where determination gets honed.

The strife inside the house and outside with the pandemic reached its apex. I had just started working minimum wage jobs and was newly back on medication when I was told I had to leave. Since leaving the hospital, I had returned to ideation seven more times, including now.

I made one desperate phone call to my youngest brother who agreed to let me stay with him. Here I was again, having to move to a new town, to escape homelessness. Detoxing off psych meds, again. As it turns out, time and distance do move the needle towards healing. Having a true safe space to finally process all the continued trauma, after four years, I was able to get out of Dante's First Circle of Hell. FINALLY. I was able to rebalance my body chemistry after the effects of the pharmaceuticals wore off. The brain fog was lifting. Clarity and sharpness were slowly returning.

I was able to land a job back in IT, working on a project improving network services. I was feeling normal again. My confidence in my knowledge and skills returned. I began teaching technology certification training at a local trade school. Now I work with artificial intelligence and autonomous vehicles, field testing them for safety before making service available to the public. I consult on the side with local and international organizations, and coach newcomers pivoting into the Internet of Things. I feel like my old self, yet am a new self altogether.

I was able to reach the shore after getting through the storm, lost in the sea of depression. After appreciating a moment on the beach in rejoice, I take more steps forward and embark on the next chapter of my life's journey. If you take a chance to try one more time, you'll get to shore too.

Greg Spiller is a multi-talented and multi-disciplined professional whose individuality and humanity shines through the prism of being a Sigma INFJ personality. Empathetic, and idealistic, independent and non-conformist, Greg forges his own path...an eternal student of Science, Art, and Philosophy, Greg's curiosity knows no bounds.

His resurrection journey of self-discovery and enlightenment was spawned from the darkest void of despair after the debilitating alienation of divorce. Greg shares his story in hopes to inspire and encourage other divorced men to endure, survive, and then thrive to overcome the odds stacked against us.

Greg is available to share his story, insights, and perspectives on a spectrum of topics. Mediums such as podcasts, speaking engagements, interviews, social media and more. You can reach and/or follow Greg here:

LinkedIn: https://www.linkedin.com/in/gregory-spiller-the-digital-diogenes-80295456

X: https://x.com/d1g1tald10genes

TIM STEINRUCK …
"KICKIN' STONES"

My name is Tim Steinruck from the Vancouver, Canada hard rock band, The Mighty One. Our song, "Kickin' Stones," is about a young man who was my best friend, and struggled with his mental health. And when life became too much eventually he ended up taking his own life. We hope that this song, "Kickin' Stones," will serve as an opportunity to talk about the reasons behind suicide and to look at the solutions, and the opportunities for suicide prevention by dialing the number 988.

Vancouver hard rock/metal band, The Mighty One, reimagines the Power Ballad for the age of social awareness.

In their 3rd album, "The Torch of Rock and Roll," The

Mighty One has chosen to go full tilt at the fragility and vulnerabilities we try to hide from all but a select few.

The 5th single from this album "Kickin' Stones", is a haunting tribute to Jeff Worobec, Tim's best friend and original drummer. The Mighty One, rounded out with talented musicians Bob Wagner (drums), Chris Campbell (bass), Randy Robertson (lead guitar) and James Meyer (keyboards) tackle the often difficult to discuss parts of what it is that makes us human, by *exploring themes of hopelessness, loneliness, isolation and suicide* in this song that also manages to remind us of the days when epic Power Ballads produced by Hard Rock and Metal bands ruled the airwaves.

"Kickin' Stones" takes you on a journey from the soft key intro to the outro that soars to instrumental heights with lyrical imagery spread evenly between. Music with a message has long existed in the genres of Hard Rock and Metal, and "Kickin' Stones" continues this tradition- delivering its message with tact and dignity while *not being afraid to say words out loud that others might bury in poetry that could obscure the fundamental message of suicide prevention and awareness.*

We were very close friends. He was a real good looking man but was famous for sabotaging his relationships. One day he came into the studio with "that" look on his face. 'What happened?' I asked. 'She's gone,' he said. 'I sent her down the road kickin' stones.' In that moment something just clicked and the story of his life became a song.

Kickin' Stones Lyrics:

Smart enough to let it go

But I don't care

'Cause I don't know

How it feels on the inside

To the end to this lovers dream

All is dead

Silent screams

Can you see it on the outside

In the bottle peace of my mind

Goin' down but I'm not the kind

Trying to get control who gives a damn

I am I am no I can't hide

Laughing crying suicide

Don't wanna face it on my own

Nooo,ohhh

No not today

Chorus:

Down the road

Kickin' stones

Kickin' them all the way

Rowboat sunrise on the lake

I could swear I felt it shake

I could use a little shaking right now

Say I'm a fool you can kiss my past

I'm living now and I'm living fast

I am the legend in my mind

I am I am whatever man

Do what I do, do what I can

An easy little problem to have

I am I am no I can't hide

Laughing crying suicide

Don't wanna face it on my own

Nooo,ohhh

No not today

Chorus

Q&A with Tim:

- Where did the band name come from?

I started The Mighty One as a solo act. The name reflects my inner power that I feel is fueled by a vast spiritual force bigger than myself that encompasses the entire universe. We are all a spark of The One.

- Is the album dedicated to Jeff?

Kickin' Stones is dedicated to Jeff. *The Torch of Rock and Roll* album is the story of my past, present and vision for the future of the band

- Are any other songs inspired by the loss of Jeff, given the titles of some of the other songs?

No, but I do explore other mental health themes in the song *Darker Side Of Me* and addiction/overdose in the song *So High*.

- Any other information, insights, or thoughts that relate to the writing of the song and the band's background?

My intention for Kickin' Stones is to spark frank conversations about suicide among youth, men and veterans to create simple solutions to a complex challenge. The Dial 988 campaign is one of them.

Call "988" The primary goal of the 988 Lifeline is to provide support for people in suicidal crisis or mental health-related distress in the moments they need it most and in a manner that is person-centered. The vast majority of those seeking help from the 988 Lifeline do not require any additional interventions at that moment. *Currently, fewer than two percent of Lifeline calls require a connection to emergency services like 911.*

We can all help prevent suicide. The 988 Lifeline provides 24/7, free and confidential support for people in distress, prevention and crisis resources for you or your loved ones, and best practices for professionals in the United States. https://988lifeline.org/

There are many reasons that people connect with the 988 Lifeline.

The 988 Lifeline responds 24/7 to calls, chats or texts from anyone who needs support for suicidal, mental health, and/or substance use crisis, and connects those in need with trained crisis counselors. Some examples in addition to thoughts of suicide are feeling overwhelmed with anxiety, sexual orientation worries, drinking too much, drug use, feeling depressed, mental and physical illness, loneliness, trauma, relationships, and economic worries.

Anyone can get broken. If someone signals distress to you, here is what you may say to help:

"It sounds like you are having a really difficult time right now. If you need a little extra emotional support, please call the 988 Suicide & Crisis Lifeline. The call is free and confidential, and crisis workers are there 24/7 to assist you. 988 is there for everyone."

"I am sorry to hear you are feeling so alone right now but hurting yourself is never the answer. There is hope and help available. Please call the 988 Suicide & Crisis Lifeline by dialing 988 or visit them online at suicidepreventionlifeline.org. They are here for you 24/7/365."

Tim Steinruck is a solo rock artist with 30+ years music and performance experience. He leads a record company, a reality television show, and an independent multi-media network. He has produced and released multiple albums of his own and for others. Tim is passionate about songwriting, performing, and supporting, and guiding independent music artists' careers.

He is also committed to the study of human psycho-spirituality and the power of discipline and purpose. His journey to becoming a certified Accelerated Evolution (TM) Success Coach not only transformed his life but also continues to transform the lives of those he serves. Armed with these priceless life lessons and gifts, Tim is committed to supporting others to create their legacy, as he continues to expand his own.

Tim's solo act and coaching website:
 https://timsteinruck.com/

The Mighty One band website:
 https://themightyone.rocks/

"The journey of a thousand miles begins with a single step"

Lao Tzu

Work and Parenting

DR ELLEN JOAN FORD …
#WORKSCHOOLHOURS

Shit, it happened again. I found myself pissed off, and I knew I had to do something about it. I don't mean the daily irritations that can come with life, I'm talking about the kind of pissed off when you realise something is so fundamentally wrong, and unfair, and systematically broken, and you know it just doesn't need to be that way - and everything in your body just launches you to do something about it.

I'm pissed off that we live in a world where parents are expected to work as though they don't have children and parent like they don't have a job. It just doesn't have to be like this. And so, unapologetically, I am terrifyingly ambitious about changing the working world.

One of the previous times I found myself pissed off was after completing my executive MBA and PhD on leadership, with the case study focused on the leadership experiences of military women. I had been lucky enough to serve the first ten years of my career as an Engineer Officer in the New Zealand Army, leading construction soldiers around the globe; rebuilding homes and infrastructure in areas impacted by war and natural disasters.

My research journey, conducted while working in the corporate sector and having my first child, revealed that while military women had plenty of positive stories to share (and we did, we really did – the wonderful camaraderie, the training and education, the opportunities to travel, to push yourself, and to help other people, to have so many amazing experiences and exciting adventures, was phenomenal!), there were however, also some recurring gender based challenges. I realised that not everything had always been the rainbows and sunshine I had so badly wanted to believe it was.

And so, I found myself pissed off. I love the military, and am so grateful for, and proud of, my military service. But I was pissed off they were not treating everyone as well as they could. And so, I had to do something about it. This led to me moonlighting in an advisory role for 18 months, providing recommendations to the Chief of the NZ Army, General John Boswell, and his senior leadership team, for positive change to benefit everyone in the organisation. Now, I can't claim to have solved the Army, but I am proud they have taken on many of my recommendations.

"To Ellen's immense credit, she has significantly influenced how the Army is now approaching a range of diversity and inclusion challenges. Her contribution has been invaluable, her expertise, interpersonal and communication skills are superb." -General Boswell

(at the orphanage)   Dr. Ellen Ford

I found myself pissed off again, almost a decade on from my military service, in August 2021, and again, I had to do something about it. The Taliban had taken over in Kabul, and as a military veteran, this was heartbreaking. But the thing I was most worried about was what was going to happen to all the people who had worked for us? You see, when I served in Afghanistan for seven months during 2010 / 2011, I had five Kiwi (NZ) soldiers in my team, and I also had 15 locals. And we were a team – if you're in my team, I'm going to love you – I lead with love. Our team of 21 worked alongside each other, we shared meals, stories, hopes and dreams – the people in my team really touched my heart.

And so, when one of my Afghan team members reached out to me in 2021, when he and his family had fled their homes, in fear of their lives, in desperation, begging me to help him, I couldn't say 'no'. I was breastfeeding my second baby at that point, caring for my three-year-old and starting my business as a keynote speaker and facilitator in the leadership space. I didn't know how to help, I didn't have the bandwidth to help, but I cared about my Afghan teammates, and I couldn't walk away.

This very quickly snowballed into the most overwhelming, monumental, draining and challenging task I had ever been involved in ever before in my life. Over the following ten months, I found myself at the heart of a volunteer team with Chris Parsons and Martin Dransfield, supported by media, generous donors, further advocates, interpreters and Government officials, all working together, to support the evacuation to New Zealand, of these Afghan workers, their wives and their children.

By July 2022, every single one of the 563 people our team secured NZ visas for, were safely in New Zealand. It was an honour to be awarded the *New Zealander of the Year – Local Hero and Person of the Year – Manawatu Standard* in recognition of what our team achieved together.

I've shared these two examples to show you that when I make statements about being terrifyingly ambitious to improve the working world, I mean it, and when I say I do something when I'm pissed off, I mean it.

And so, here I was again, pissed off. Pissed off that we live in a world where we are expected to work as though we don't have children and parent like we don't have a job. And so, I am doing something about this. Not something to change parents or change children, but changing the system that creates this ridiculous juggle.

I remember the moment clearly: I was on parental leave from my business consulting job for the second time. It was the middle of the night, maybe one or two in the morning. I was breastfeeding my baby, Monty, and I was marinating, really stewing, on the data from my post-doctoral research which focused on the experiences of working parents.

Hundreds and hundreds of parents had reached out to me (I now have qualitative data and stories from well over a thousand parents around the globe, across a variety of industries), wanting to share their experiences of being a working parent. This wasn't a planned research project, but when I kept hearing the same stories over and over, I kind of couldn't help myself from taking a note of what they were saying. The stories these parents shared fit into one of three categories.

Category one was the parents who couldn't make work, work. And when I say 'work,' I am referring to paid work, because there is a whole ton of unpaid work done in the home. Furthermore, I am not referring to parents who consciously choose to be solely focused on their children – the parents in this category wanted to work but couldn't make the juggle of being in the paid workforce alongside the responsibilities of caring for children, work. In many cases, the cost of childcare just didn't stack up when it came to what they would be able to earn in the workforce.

One particular story, which of course, wasn't just one story, it was the story of many parents, really moved me. A young solo mother shared how she was excited to be offered her first job. Being in the workforce meant so much to her; for her identity, for her satisfaction in life, for how she wanted to be a role model to her children, for her future and for theirs. But when she talked me through the logistics, she would have to leave home before eight in the morning and wouldn't get home again until after six in the evening. With two young school children, and a minimum wage job, there was no way she could afford the before and after school childcare that would be required. She had no option but to decline the job offer and stay on a welfare benefit. "I can't see any other options for at least the next decade," she sobbed. My own eyes welled up; here was a woman excluded from the workforce because the current construct of work clashes frustratingly with the fact she is a parent.

The second category of parents worked full time and lamented the moments they missed with their children. They couldn't pick their kids up from school, didn't get to hang out with the kids during the school holidays, and couldn't attend the cross-country and school athletics days. One mother, whose children had grown up, burst into tears, "I can't get that time back, it's too late now. I worked my butt off, constantly feeling judged when I had to take a day off when the kids were sick, missing so much of their childhood, and for what? To work for some asshole who really didn't give a shit about me!"

Category number three were parents who approached me not to whinge, but to tell me how lucky they were to be an exception. These were the parents who worked part time so they could spend more time with their children. At first glance, this seemed like a great balance. However, when I sought to understand how this played out, the conversation to initiate a part time contract almost always went something like this:

"Hey boss, I'd like to scale back my hours to spend more time with the kids."

The boss would either say, "no," in which case, categories one or two became the outcome. Or, the boss would respond with, "yes, sure thing, happy to support that, just as long as you get all your work done." Just as long as you get all your work done…

So, these parents would get all their work done. Often working beyond their paid hours, but most prominently, they just became more efficient, and got their work done in less time. Their contracts would be amended; less hours and less pay. Many of these parents were on 25- or 30-hour contracts, and yet still delivering the same outputs as their full time colleagues. These parents told me how lucky they were. "Oh Ellen, I am so fortunate to be allowed to work part time… I'm so grateful that my boss permits me to work fewer hours." Of course, these 'lucky' situations came with career caps to their progression, being overlooked for promotions, and a general sense from their colleagues and managers that being part time meant they were less dedicated and less committed than their full time peers.

When I kept hearing the word 'lucky,' over and over, this is where my rage really set in!

There is nothing lucky about getting a pay cut to do the same job.

This is societal wide gaslighting!

None of these outcomes were ok to me. I love my kids, I also love the work I do delivering keynotes on leadership and facilitating workshops to lift leadership capabilities. I don't want to be with my kids 24/7 and I also know for me personally, I am a better mother because I work. But I also don't want to work all the hours and miss the moments that matter with my kids. So, categories one and two are not for me. And as for category three, well, I am sure as shit not going to take a pay cut to do the same job.

And so there I was, breastfeeding Monty in the early hours, feeling pissed off again, knowing I had to do something about it. I don't want this for my life ahead and I don't want it for other people, either.

At that moment, after allowing myself an hour or so for a pity party, I stopped wallowing. I put on my big girl panties and knew I had to change the working world. I knew I had to change the system, change the construct of work, to normalise that people can be highly successful as both parents and professionals. Because if I didn't do something about this, I would either have to spend less time with my children, or I'd have to trick myself into thinking I am ok with lowering my expectations around career success. I just don't want to do either of those. I want to have my cake and eat it, too.

Because what the heck is the point of having cake if you can't also eat it?!!

Over the following months, which, incidentally, was happening at the same time as the Afghanistan evacuation volunteer task, I started furiously putting together everything I knew about leadership and organisational performance; from my own experiences leading in the military and corporate sector, and my research on leadership, to find a better way.

This is how the #WorkSchoolHours movement was born.

Now, before you write this off as some dogmatic idea that would 'never work in the real world' (yes, I have been told that multiple times), please just give me a couple more pages of your time, and remember that practical outcomes and pragmatism are part of my story; this is not just some lovely 'pie in the sky' idea, there is a business case to this.

Before sharing more about what #WorkSchoolHours is, and isn't, let me very quickly share with you how the problem requiring #WorkSchoolHours came about. So, the 9-5, or the 40-hour week was really cemented in our society more than a century ago, in line with Henry Ford's car manufacturing era. This was fantastic social progress at that time. But the 9-5 construct was built on the assumption that every household had a dedicated worker, a man, and a dedicated caregiver of children, a woman. The person who was working 9-5 was not the same person who was collecting the kids from school in the afternoons and caring for the kids during the school holidays.

However, women have been in the workforce en masse for decades now. We didn't just rock up in 2024 – we have been here many generations now! It was as though women were 'allowed' to join the workforce, so long as they still took care of all the domestic duties, as well.

We have had so many incredible transformations in our society over the past century, and it blows my mind that the construct of work has not been one of them.

I mean honestly, if we had a blank slate today and were thinking about the best way to structure work, only a complete moron would conclude that we should put adults on one schedule and children on a different schedule. The current construct is absolutely bonkers!

But it doesn't have to be this way. And this is what gets me really excited. Making things better for parents, in a way that makes things better for everyone, is also good for business. Here's why:

#WorkSchoolHours is a set of principles derived from my overarching leadership model of Belonging, Autonomy and Purpose. I believe that a leader's job is to create an environment where their team can thrive and then direct that thriving energy at the task that needs to be achieved. What do people need to thrive?

They need a sense of belonging, where they can show up as their whole, full, authentic, diverse, unique, a little bit weird, self, and feel they are truly valued and included. People don't like to be micromanaged; they need a sense of agency, or autonomy, over how, and if possible, when and where, they conduct their tasks. And further, people need to know that what they do matters – they need a sense of purpose.

When people have a sense of belonging, autonomy and purpose, I tell you what, they thrive, they do their best work, they have their best experiences, and they deliver the best outcomes for their organisations. I know this through my military leadership journey, leading in the corporate world, my MBA, PhD and post-doctoral research journey, and through becoming a parent. But my very best case study, which I didn't realise until afterwards, was the Afghan evacuation task. Our team had belonging, autonomy and purpose, and because of this, we achieved a complex task with an exceedingly low likelihood of success; it truly felt like a miracle.

But working parents don't have a full sense of belonging. It's as though we can be at work, provided we hide as much as possible the fact we are also a parent, meaning we aren't actually welcomed to bring our whole self to work. Our autonomy is impacted when we are expected to work until 5pm and also do school collection at 3pm, working approximately 48 weeks of the year, but caring for our children for roughly 13 weeks of school holidays. **Our two purposes (be a good parent and be a good worker) are in constant conflict.**

The impact of this reduced sense of belonging, autonomy and purpose means that working parents are limited in their ability to thrive, which negatively impacts theirs and their family's experiences. It also hampers their ability to do their best work for their organisations. **The stress, the constant parent guilt and the impossible juggle has a huge impact on mental health.**

When we realise that roughly 80 percent of the population become parents at some point, and even if people choose not to have children themselves, as a human race, we do need people to breed to continue the human race, we can see what a truly astronomical problem this is for our world.

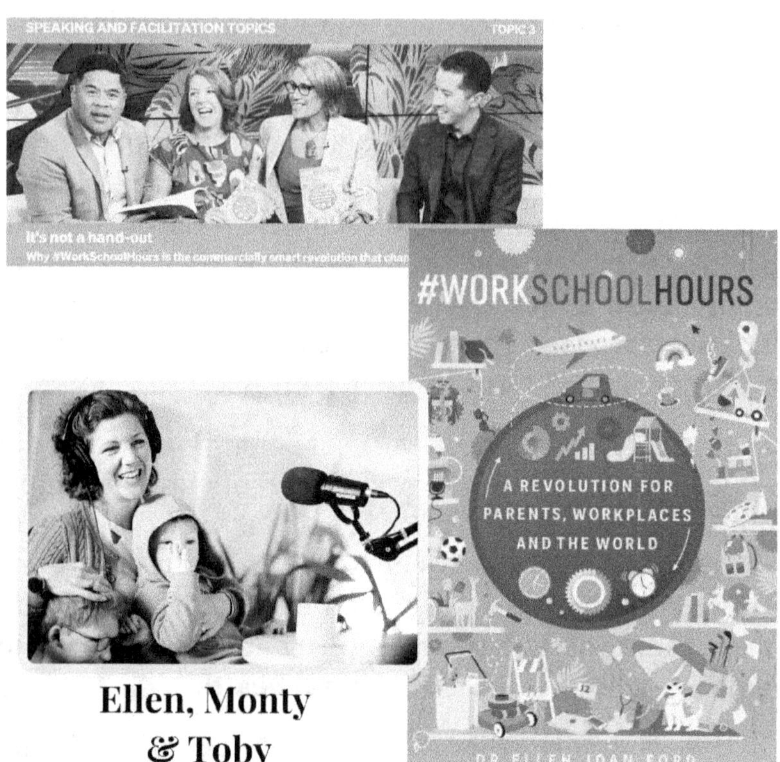

Ellen, Monty & Toby

So #WorkSchoolHours looks to increase this sense of belonging, autonomy and purpose for parents, to improve both social and commercial outcomes. #WorkSchoolHours is based on three principles.

Firstly, organisations should do more to value the fact that people have things they care about outside of work. This may be children; the challenges facing working parents was absolutely the genesis for #WorkSchoolHours. But guess what? Everyone has things they care about outside of work. My incredible little brother, who doesn't have kids, is an Ironman (yes, I am bragging about how insanely proud

I am of Ewen), and he talked about how wonderful it would be to conduct his training during daylight hours. Additionally, we have an aging population with more workers responsible for caring for elderly relatives. When it comes to disabilities and neurodiversity, there are more and more people for whom the 8-hour day is not serving.

The second principle is to focus on outputs, what it is we want our people to deliver, instead of caring so much about their inputs, their hours and location of work. When leaders employ new members into their teams it's because they want X, Y and Z tasks completed. So why is it that as soon as the contract is signed, we then manage people based on the hours they are working? If someone can complete their work in less than 40 hours, which is the case for so many parents working part time, we should be rewarding their efficiency, not cutting their pay and limiting their career progression. This absolutely applies to leaders, too.

A leader's job is to create an environment where their team can thrive, where they have belonging, autonomy and purpose, and then direct that thriving energy at the task that needs to be achieved. Nothing in that job description suggests the leader must work a set number of hours to achieve that. Outputs are what really matters.

The third principle is to give people more flexibility where possible. I don't mean that we let a surgeon walk out mid-operation at 2:30pm to do the school pick-up. It astounds me how often this example is suggested to me by a smug audience member who can't wait to tell me the issues with #WorkSchoolHours. For the record, I know this – I am not a complete idiot.

> *#WorkSchoolHours is about applying the three principles where we can, to enhance the sense of belonging, autonomy and purpose for everyone.*

And how those principles are applied looks different in every team, organisation, role and industry. My book, not surprisingly titled, #WorkSchoolHours: A Revolution for Parents, Workplaces and the World, along with my self-paced online courses (an edition for parents, and an edition for people leaders) is packed with practical examples from a variety of industries for how to apply these principles to make tangible improvements; professional services, healthcare, construction, transport, farming, manufacturing, shift workers and more. *I have yet to deliver a workshop for an organisation that was not able to make positive change by applying the #WorkSchoolHours principles in some way.*

This may look like moving all team meetings to be within the school day, scheduling projects around the school term, ensuring team training days are not during the school holidays, finishing in time for school collection one day per fortnight, or going 'all in' and truly encouraging the team to deliver their outputs when it works for them, in and around the other commitments in their lives. Any movement along the spectrum is positive.

Leaders don't need to come up with all the solutions – get the team to do it. Literally tell your team, "These are the outputs we need to achieve as a team, how might we do this differently?" **You might be surprised how creative people can be at finding efficiencies when they are sufficiently motivated by the ability to go home**

earlier. And the benefits to organisations are significant! Improved productivity, better staff well-being, improved attraction and retention of great talent (staff attrition is a huge cost for organisations), and better representation of women in senior leadership positions; all of which improves overall organisational performance and the bottom line. The principles of #WorkSchoolHours just make sense!

I knew deep within me that this message was needed, is needed, for our world. So, since late 2021, I have been frantically writing and submitting articles to publications around the world. Initially, 90-ish percent ignored me, 9-ish percent said "no," and then 1

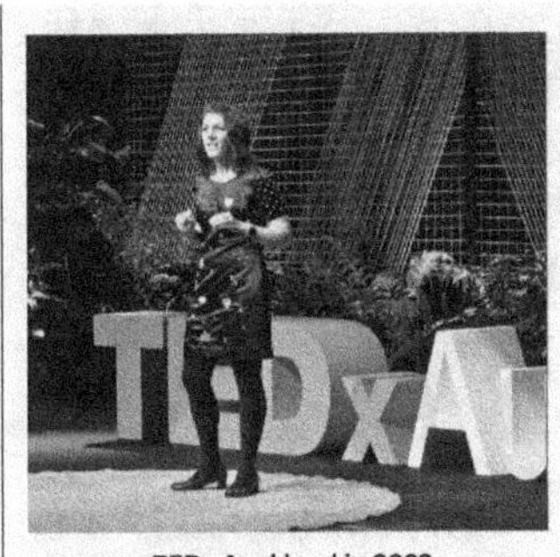

TEDx Auckland in 2022

This event showcased her expertise and commitment to driving positive change in the workplace.

percent would publish my work. Likewise, I started pitching to mainstream media, podcasts and posting on social media. I stalked TEDx organisers on LinkedIn until TEDx Auckland, New Zealand's largest TEDx event, agreed to let me talk on the red circle.

And I'm excited. Three years on and the #WorkSchoolHours movement is gaining momentum. I've published my book (**endorsed as commercially smart** by multiple business leaders – one of my favourites from the giant, EY, "even the sceptic in me is totally convinced"), released two self-paced online courses, am being booked more and more to deliver international keynotes and workshops on leadership. My work has been published multiple times around the world, am guesting on more and more podcasts, and #WorkSchoolHours has featured in numerous media outlets, including TV, magazines, national radio, business subscriptions, newspapers and more. It was an honour to receive the prestigious Sir Peter Blake Leadership Award for my efforts to change the working world.

There is more to be done. I haven't changed the working world yet, but I know it can be better than it is. I have more and more organisational examples to prove that the principles of #WorkSchoolHours is good for business.

I've always believed that if you want to change the world, you have to change people's hearts. And this is why #WorkSchoolHours and Belonging, Autonomy and Purpose matters.

My little boys, Toby, seven and Monty, four, mean the world to me. And while no parent can honestly say they have their shit sorted (I don't), as a single mum, running my own business, I am there for the majority of the school pick-ups, school holiday periods are mostly with my kids, I get to almost all of the school events such as swimming sports, and I spend Fridays with Monty. Often, when I travel for work, I bring one, or both of my kids along – we have adventures together around the world. This stuff makes my life so meaningful. I like that my kids see their Mum at work, too. I let my clients know my kids will be coming to the meeting or event, without apologising, and no one has ever had an issue with it.

We all need to keep challenging the status quo. The current construct of work, the status quo of the 9-5, is not serving us well, so let's do something about it.

I want all working parents to know their value. Talk to your boss about how you want to add value to the organisation, while also attending to the things you care about outside of work. Frame it as a win-win, not as a problem for them to solve. "I'm going to deliver these great outputs for you, I just need to structure my work a little differently." Derisk it for your boss by suggesting a trial with an evaluation and do your best work. Make it really hard for your boss to say "no."

A Dad emailed me recently to say, "I attended my son's athletics last week for the first time ever. I can't express how much I cherished this moment. Thank you for showing me things could be different."

If any of this resonates, join the #WorkSchoolHours movement. My book, TEDx talk, online courses, speaker reel and plenty more resources are available on my website: www.workschoolhours.com and you can follow on social media: Dr Ellen Joan Ford.

But don't just follow my work, **please do something**. Share your stories using the hashtag #WorkSchoolHours, share this content with your friends and family, and influence your workplaces. Together, we can change the working world.

Dr Ellen Joan Ford is terrifyingly ambitious about her **mission to improve the working world for people and for organisations.**

As a leader, researcher, military veteran, international speaker, TEDx speaker, facilitator, and parent, Ellen draws on her research and practical experiences to drive organisational outcomes by enhancing inclusive leadership capabilities and workplace culture; giving people better experiences at work. Her keynotes and workshops are full of practical takeaways.

Ellen was awarded the *Kiwi Bank New Zealander of the Year - Local Hero, Person of the Year -* Manawatu Standard and the prestigious *Sir Peter Blake Leadership Award.*

She is the author of #WorkSchoolHours (endorsed by CEOs of KiwiBank, FMG, DevryBV and Cliftons, and dubbed a "must-read for any leader building a modern workplace") and her leadership model is Belonging, Autonomy and Purpose.

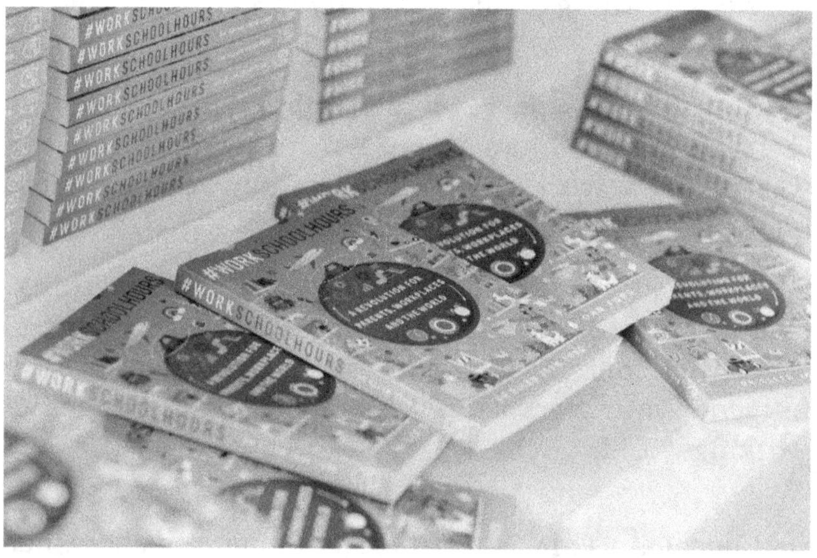

Ellen is passionate, authentic and speaks from the heart with warmth, enthusiasm, bubbliness and fun. www.ellenjoanford.com | https://www.linkedin.com/in/dr-ellen-joan-ford-791a2655/

Beating All the Odds

BRI CAMPANO ... HOW PODCASTING SAVED MY LIFE

The voice screamed in my head, relentless and unyielding. "Get Up, get up, get up! You can't sit there any longer!" It wasn't a gentle nudge or a friendly suggestion. No, this was a full-blown, no-holds-barred assault on my self-pity. And let me tell you, I needed it. I needed it like a kick in the ass from a steel-toed boot.

You see, I was drowning. Not in water, but in a sea of my own despair. Two pulmonary embolisms, a clot in my leg, heart failure, and a bad heart valve. It reads like a medical textbook's greatest hits, doesn't it? A litany of health issues that could make even the most optimistic person want to curl up in a ball and cry uncle. And that's exactly what I was doing.

But that voice... that damn voice wouldn't let me be. It kept hammering away at the walls I'd built around myself. "You're ok with this? You're going to just sit there and accept this? This? You can honestly look me in the eye and tell me you're just going to do nothing?"

I wanted to scream back, to tell it to shut up and leave me alone. But deep down, I knew it was right. I knew I was better than this. I knew I had more fight in me. But knowing something and doing something about it are two very different beasts.

The voice continued its tirade, each word a dagger of truth. "Is that what you want? Is that what your family would want? Your friends? Don't kid me. I know you better than anyone. Don't just sit there any longer, get up and fight!"

And there it was. The challenge. The gauntlet was thrown down at my feet. Fight. Such a simple word, but in that moment, it felt like the hardest thing in the world.

Let me paint you a picture of where I was at that point. Imagine waking up every day, not to the chirping of birds or the gentle rays of sunlight, but to a crushing weight on your chest. A weight made up of fear, uncertainty, and the gnawing question of "Will this be my last day?" That was my reality.

I couldn't even plan what to have for dinner. Can you believe that? Something so mundane, so everyday, had become an insurmountable task. Because planning for dinner meant planning for a future, and in my mind, that future didn't exist.

For two whole months, I sat in this pit of despair. Two months of going through the motions, of existing but not living. Two months of letting everything fall by the wayside. Bills piled up, unanswered. Groceries became an afterthought. The simple joys of life? They might as well have been on another planet.

But then, something happened. A tiny, almost imperceptible shift. A flicker of light in the darkness. You know how they say we're drawn to shiny things? Well, this wasn't shiny. It was more like a spark. A tiny ember of possibility that somehow managed to catch my eye.

Podcasting. Of all the things in the world, it was podcasting that became my lifeline. Crazy, right? Here I was, barely able to get out of bed, and suddenly I'm thinking about starting a podcast. It was new, it was scary, and it was so far outside my comfort zone that I might as well have been on Mars.

But here's the thing about hitting rock bottom: the only way left to go is up. And podcasting? It gave me a direction. It gave me something to focus on that wasn't my failing health or my uncertain future.

I threw myself into it with a fervor that surprised even me. I learned everything I could about it. I practiced, I stumbled, I failed, and then I got back up and tried again. And you know what? It felt good. For the first time in months, I felt a spark of excitement, a glimmer of purpose.

Now, let me be clear. My health hadn't magically improved. The embolisms were still there, my heart was still a mess, and every day was still a struggle. But my outlook? That had changed. And sometimes, that's all you need to start turning things around.

As I delved deeper into the world of podcasting, I started to notice something. Thursdays became special. Not because of any podcast-related event, but because of the mindset it put me in. I started calling it my "possibility day."

You see, on Thursdays, we're close enough to the weekend to start thinking about it, but not so close that we're just rushing to get there. It's a day of planning, of dreaming, of opening our minds to what could be. And that mindset of possibility? It started seeping into other areas of my life.

I began to ask myself, "What if?" What if I could do that thing I've always wanted to do? What if I could make a difference? What if I stopped focusing on what was happening to me and started thinking about what I could make happen?

It wasn't an overnight transformation. Far from it. There were still days when getting out of bed felt like climbing Mount Everest. Days when the voice of doubt was louder than the voice of possibility. But I kept pushing. I kept podcasting. **I kept believing that maybe, just maybe, there was more to my story than a tragic medical case.** I began not one but two podcasts. The first, a conversation with some captivating humans and the other, a total guilty pleasure on my favorite TV show. Before long I was coaching others to launch their podcasts and producing shows with top talent in the industry. I don't know how I did it all, I just grabbed every possibility that came my way and ran with it. Life, it seemed, was turning out pretty ok. Or so I thought.

And then came the bombshell. A CT scan revealed a tear in my aorta. "Life-threatening" doesn't even begin to cover it. Most people with this condition don't even make it to the hospital. They're not upright, they're not conscious, they're certainly not walking and talking.

But there I was, strolling into the ER like I was there for a routine check-up. The doctors were baffled. They couldn't understand how I was even functioning. And to be honest, neither could I.

Emergency open-heart surgery followed. It was terrifying, it was risky, and it was absolutely necessary. But you want to know the craziest part? That night, after my surgery, I was dancing. Yes, you read that right. *Dancing.* The nurses told me I needed to stand and walk a bit, and in true rebellious fashion, I decided to take it a step further.

Was it smart? Probably not. Was it reckless? Almost certainly. But in that moment, it felt like a victory...a middle finger to the universe that had tried to keep me down. I danced, and I laughed, and for the first time in a long time, I felt truly alive.

The doctors later told me something that still gives me chills. My aorta had folded on top of my heart, sealing the tear that should have killed me. It was a one-in-a-million occurrence. A miracle, if you believe in such things. And you know what? After everything I'd been through, I was starting to.

Throughout this entire ordeal, my passion for podcasting never wavered. In fact, it grew stronger. I became known as the "podcasting lady" in my circles. People started coming to me for advice and help launching their own shows. I loved every minute of it.

I saw it as my mission to help others find their voice, to share their stories with the world.

If my journey had taught me anything, it was that our

stories have power. They have the ability to connect us, to inspire us, to show us that we're not alone in our struggles.

My vision expanded. I didn't just want to help people in my local community or even just in my country. I wanted to teach podcasting around the world. I believed, with every fiber of my being, that if we could share our stories globally, if we could foster understanding across cultures and borders; we could make the world a better place.

Was it a lofty goal? Absolutely. Was it maybe a bit naive? Probably. But after staring death in the face and coming out the other side, I wasn't interested in small dreams anymore.

Now, here I am, ten weeks post-surgery, and sometimes I forget I even had the operation. My business is thriving, and growing in ways I never imagined possible. Even during my month-long recovery in the hospital, it continued to expand. **It's as if the universe is saying, "See? This is what happens when you don't give up."**

But let me be clear - this isn't a story about smooth sailing and easy victories. It's a story of struggle, of doubt, of moments when giving up seemed like the only option. It's a story of imperfection and mistakes, of days when the voice of possibility was drowned out by the screams of fear and uncertainty.

There were times when I pushed too hard, when my body reminded me in no uncertain terms that I wasn't invincible; times when my passion bordered on obsession, when I neglected other important aspects of my life in pursuit of my goals.

I'm not perfect. Far from it. I'm stubborn to a fault, often pushing myself beyond my limits. I'm impatient, wanting results now rather than later. And sometimes, in my eagerness to help others, I forget to take care of myself.

But you know what? I'm okay with that. Because these flaws, these imperfections - they're part of what makes me who I am. They're part of what drove me to fight when everything seemed hopeless. They're part of what makes my story real, and raw, and hopefully, relatable.

And let me tell you, this journey? It's not for the faint of heart. It's for the fighters, the dreamers, the ones who refuse to let life beat them down. But here's the kicker - we're all capable of being that person. Yes, even you, sitting there thinking, "Not me. I'm not strong enough." Trust me, you are.

You want to know the secret? *It's not about being fearless. It's about being scared out of your mind and doing it anyway. It's about shaking in your boots but taking that step forward. Because here's the truth - courage isn't the absence of fear. It's action in the face of it.*

I remember the first time I sat down to record a podcast. My hands were shaking so bad I could barely hold the microphone. My voice? It quivered like a leaf in a storm. And don't even get me started on the cold sweat. I was a mess.

But you know what? I did it anyway. I stumbled through that first recording like a newborn giraffe trying to walk. It was awkward, it was messy, and if I'm being honest, it was pretty terrible. But it was a start. And sometimes, that's all we need.

Now, I'm not going to sit here and tell you that everything

magically fell into place after that. Life doesn't work that way, and anyone who tells you otherwise is selling something. There were plenty of times when I wanted to quit, when the tech issues or the self-doubt or the sheer exhaustion of it all made me want to throw in the towel.

But each time I felt like giving up, I remembered that voice. The one that had pulled me out of my despair in the first place. And I'd ask myself, "Is this really where you want to stop? Is this really the end of your story?"

And every single time, the answer was a resounding "Hell no!"

Because here's the thing about passion - it's not always comfortable. In fact, most of the time, it's downright uncomfortable. It pushes you, challenges you, forces you to confront parts of yourself you'd rather ignore. But that discomfort? That's where the growth happens.

I've made mistakes along the way. Plenty of them. I've put my foot in my mouth more times than I can count. I've given advice that, looking back, makes me cringe. I've had technical difficulties that made me want to throw my equipment out the window.

But each mistake, each stumble, each face-plant into the metaphorical dirt? It taught me something. It made me better. Not just as a podcaster, but as a person.

And that's the beauty of embracing your passion, of chasing your dreams. It's not just about achieving a goal. It's about who you become in the process.

Now, let's talk about fear for a moment. Because if you're thinking about taking that leap, about chasing your own passion, I can guarantee you one thing - fear will be right there with you. It'll whisper in your ear, telling you all the ways you could fail, all the reasons you're not good enough.

But here's a little secret I've learned: fear is a liar. It's a storyteller that specializes in worst-case scenarios and what-ifs. And the only way to shut it up? Action.

Every time you take a step forward, every time you do the thing that scares you, you're proving fear wrong. You're showing it that its stories don't define you. You're the author of your own tale, and you get to decide how it unfolds.

Of course, it's not always easy to remember that when you're in the thick of it. There have been nights when I've lain awake, my mind racing with all the ways things could go wrong; mornings when the weight of my ambitions felt too heavy to bear.

But in those moments, I've learned to be gentle with myself. To acknowledge the fear, the doubt, the uncertainty - and then to keep going anyway. Because at the end of the day, I'd rather live with the discomfort of pushing my boundaries than the regret of playing it safe.

And let me tell you, the view from outside your comfort zone? It's pretty spectacular.

Now, I know what some of you might be thinking: "That's all well and good for you, but my situation is different. I have responsibilities, limitations, obstacles you can't even imagine."

To that, I say - you're absolutely right. Your situation

is unique. Your challenges are your own. But here's the thing - so are your strengths, your experiences, your perspective. And those? They're your superpowers.

The world doesn't need another carbon copy success story. It needs your story, told in your voice, with all its quirks and imperfections and beautiful, messy humanity.

Because here's the truth - we're all flawed. We're all struggling with something. And it's in sharing those struggles, in being vulnerable and real, that we connect with others. That we inspire. That we make a difference.

So whatever your passion is, whatever that little voice inside you is urging you to do - listen to it. Give it a chance. It doesn't have to be perfect. It doesn't have to change the world overnight. It just has to be authentic. It just has to be you.

And who knows? Maybe your story, your journey, will be the spark that ignites someone else's flame of possibility. Maybe your courage will give someone else the strength to take that first step.

Because in the end, that's what it's all about. It's about lifting each other up, about creating a ripple effect of possibility and hope. It's about showing the world that no matter how dark things might seem, there's always a flicker of light if you're willing to look for it.

So here's my final challenge to you: Take that step. Make that leap. Embrace your passion with everything you've got. Be messy, be imperfect, be gloriously, unapologetically you.

Because the world needs your voice. It needs your story. It needs your unique brand of magic.

And trust me, once you start living your truth, once you start chasing your dreams with everything you've got? That's when the real adventure begins. That's when you discover what you're truly capable of.

So what are you waiting for? Your story is out there, waiting to be lived. Your passion is calling, waiting to be embraced. And the world? It's ready for you, in all your imperfect, passionate, incredible glory. Are you ready to start that podcast?

Get up. Get moving. Get living. Because this is your time. This is your moment. And I, for one, can't wait to see what you do with it.

Remember, the journey of a thousand miles begins with a single step. So take that step. And then another. And another. Before you know it, you'll be running towards your dreams, fear and doubt eating your dust.

And when you get there? When you're standing on the mountaintop of your own success, looking back at the path you've traveled? That's when you'll realize - it was worth it. Every struggle, every setback, every moment of doubt. It was all worth it.

Because you didn't just achieve a goal. You became the person you were always meant to be. And that, my friends, is the greatest victory of all.

So go ahead. Write your story. Live your passion. Change your world. Because if there's one thing I know for sure, it's this - you've got greatness inside you. All you have to do is let it out.

Now get out there and show the world what you're made of. I'll be cheering you on every step of the way.

Bri Campano, is a podcast host, producer, and coach who's passionate about helping people find their voice in the podcasting world. There's nothing she enjoys more than watching someone turn their ideas into a powerful podcast.

Bri hosts several podcasts, "Clever Conversations," "Spill the ImmuniTEA" (where are my Survivor fans?), and "Discovering Greatness." She has also produced shows starring Shari Belafonte, Jason George, Gordon Firemark, and Elsie Escobar.

Bri believes in helping podcasters around the world create and launch their own podcasts. We can all learn more about each other and make the world a kinder place.

IG https://www.instagram.com/thecleverbiotch/

YouTube https://www.youtube.com/ @BEYONDREACHSTUDIOS

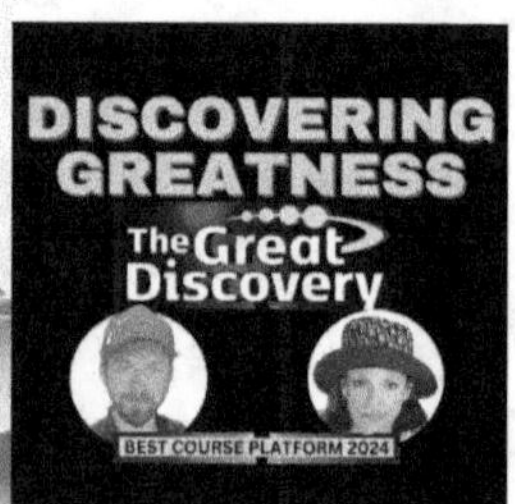

Delight in Your Own Power to Create

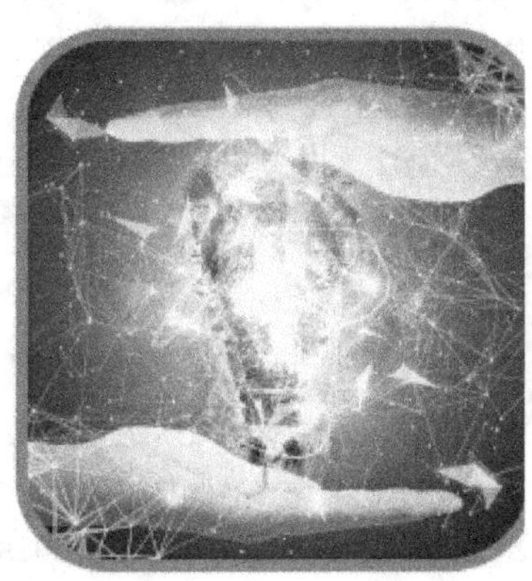

LONNEE REY … CAR ACCIDENTS AND MOVING FORWARD

The sound of tires screeching was an uh-ohhh; the sound of a car's impact following it, horrifying. You could tell it was *bad*. I jumped to the window, and watched a toddler running across his yard. Neither he, nor anyone sitting at the yard sale, was injured. Ohh thank God! And then I saw it: tracks across grass, skid marks on two trees, and a young male passenger hopping out of his window. *Holy shit.* I ran downstairs and across the street to see if I could help. IDK why because the sight of blood makes me weak. As a chiropractic assistant, however, I knew enough to stop him from yanking her from the car.

"DON'T MOVE HER!!" I yelled repeatedly as I ran toward their car. It didn't matter: he'd seen too many movies and thought the car was going to blow-up. He insisted on moving her to the ground. "Oh God," I thought. Just how this 90-lb girl survived, I'll never know. I assured her everything would be alright. Hovering over her on the ground, the best help I could be was to shade her eyes from the sun *and keep her talking*. Please don't pass out on me, Honey.

In 2012, just after being "excused" from Australia thanks to a careless sponsor, I was stressed, tired, working far too many hours and trying to recover from the move back to South Carolina. The sunset was in my eyes, and I failed to see the other guy, gunning it to make the light, too. I heard the horn, but it was too late: I drove right into his work van, causing a head-on collision so bad we bounced and hit each other twice, locking front ends.

The only person who stood by me was a curious little girl who stared at me from the open car door. "Go away," I breathlessly said. "Stop staring at me." The sheer shock of it all will take your breath away, let alone breaking your body. The body and mind can't correlate what's happened because everything is shaken-up. It's confusing, like any 'sucker punch' would be. There aren't any tears; the body can't even figure out the extent of damage. However, trauma sets in immediately. Hearing the sirens that day, I knew it was bad. It would be weeks before I could actually, physically, cry.

Compounding injuries from the accident as well as that forced move back to the U.S. really took a toll on my plans to restart life. I was a wreck in more ways than one. Seven fractured ribs, a cracked sternum, a broken foot and a boxer's break, not to mention multiple bruises, really messed me up. I'd hurt someone else, too. That it was my fault only added to the mental anguish. That he worked for the same company I did was a dose of salt on a huge wound. *Gawd.*

Getting over an accident takes more time than you can imagine. Driving is unnerving for at least a year. Dreams of the smoking engine, the toxic odors, the sounds of brakes and tires squealing, then the horrific sounds of impact, tend to stick around for far too long. It's reliving your worst day against your will. "The smell of the engine will pass," my mother said. "It took me about a year. And it takes longer to not be paranoid every time you drive, but you'll get there." She was right on both accounts. Eventually, I was back to driving and the accident was long-forgotten, aided by the 'wipe' of an "at-fault accident" from my insurance. The increase in costs lasted years – a penalty-box reminder that only made the accident remain top-of-mind. Not helpful. Insurance companies know a person will be involved in a second accident more often than not, btw. There is a high rate of probability. Even so, it's not a jinx you want, stat or no stat. It only adds to your burden of recovery. Hyper vigilance will wear you out.

It takes distance from an event to get right side up again...just as it does in life. Sitting 'courtside' to this crazy accident, right outside my window, brought back so many memories. If she lived, she was going to have a tough road ahead.

"It'll be OK," I told the featherweight young lady. Was I convincing enough? "Don't worry. No, no, keep your eyes open, Sweetie. Stay awake. Help is coming. Lay still. Your friend is OK, babe. You were in an accident, is all. They will be here in a minute – STAY AWAKE, BABY." Thankfully, she did.

"No LOC," I told the paramedics. LOC, Loss of Consciousness, ramps up the severity and expediency of treatment. It does not mean she was free of severe internal injuries, however.

"What about him?" the officer said, gesturing to the passenger. "He didn't lose consciousness at all. In fact, he climbed out the passenger window and moved her with no problem."

Declining an ambulance, or a ride from me back home, he phoned a friend and I waited with him. Then, I trotted back to my desk, shaking. I felt so grateful the toddler didn't get struck as her car whizzed past his tiny body. The second tree she hit stopped her car from barreling into the house itself. It could have been so much worse for everybody.

That afternoon, driving all of 1.5 miles to the grocery store, I witnessed another car accident. It would have been me, had the woman not pulled into the lane right in front of me. The same red-headed cop I'd spoken to two hours before arrived on the scene. What are the odds? "Are the kids OK?" he said. "Yes, just really shaken, sir." There was no consoling the tykes. I gave him my report and slowly drove away. What a day.

I've traveled thousands of miles, taken one-way trips to explore Alaska and Australia, even, without a single incident or accident. That two occurred right in front of me, on the same day, was unbelievable "luck."

Seeing, let alone being in an accident, changes a person. It is a form of trauma; it can become an insidious memory and emotional trigger. Thought field therapy, created by

Dr. Roger Callahan, proved it: with every thought there is an energy field associated with it. If there is an emotional response, such as stress, anxiety, tears, or panic, Dr. Callahan's research proved there to be a perturbation, or 'blowout' in the circular flow of energy. His creation, now popularly known as "tapping," is like Fix-A-Flat for emotional blowouts. It heals the perturbation (think "perturbed") thanks to acupressure point stimulation. Here is my video of the 5-minute routine, developed by students of Dr. Callahan, which will help *if you use it*. I also found it helps with procrastination: *"Tap Happy: 'Fix-a-Flat for Emotional Blowouts' with Lonnee Rey"* https://youtu.be/Q8yVih75Wc4?si=Gtp1hjsy1IfHvGUV

"My life story includes staying in battered women & homeless shelters. While there, I shared this technique with a woman who was STUCK. Days later, she came to me with little bruises on her face, at the points demonstrated for tapping. "Oh, what happened?" She smiled at me and said, "I've got a LOT of issues and feel MUCH better now, thank you so much." We both had a laugh about it. This really works and, unlike traditional talk therapy where the patient is re-traumatized in reliving their story (yes, it has value to be heard, but) tapping helps by releasing the emotional tie to the story. Like gravity, it works whether you believe in it or not...and the patient doesn't have to tell me their story...they only need to think about a particular thought and do the simple tapping routine until the 'stress rating' decreases to a 1 or two."

In spite of the driving-related 'events,' I still drive a car.

Sure, the 2nd-degree burn scar on my chest (airbags are rock hard and hot as hell!) reminds me of that horrible head-on crash only every single day. People notice it and look away. I get it. The same thing happens now with my distorted hand. Oh well.

> *Shit happens. F it. Seriously: add an "F"*
> *to the same word and you get shiFt.*

No matter what has happened to you, honey, you just keep on driving, ok? "Tap" your way back to neutral and hit the gas 'cuz bumps and battle wounds are going to happen along the way. Don't let these incidents stop you from moving forward with your life. They can mess with your mind but that does not need to become your new mindset. You've got things to do and past events are no reason to sit in fear of what *might* happen.

Let LOL = Live Out Loud from now on!

I hope this will help remind you of a time when you did the "impossible" because I know you did – we all have:

Think back to when you needed to walk across a five-lane road. Remember how you stepped off the curb once the traffic was clear on your side, and you probably had to pause in the center lane? Standing there, waiting for traffic to clear, you set your sights on the goal: the other side of the road. What happened next? Did a 'hole' open up? Or maybe the drivers saw you, slowed down and waved you past them? Something happened that enabled you to reach the other side, right? Well, if you never stepped off that curb, the opening wouldn't have had to happen at all. No one would have stopped to allow you to pass. Why would they if you were standing still?

*"Whatever you can do, or dream
you can do, begin it. Boldness has
genius, power, and magic in it."*

(This phrase is often attributed to Goethe, but its source is actually William Hutchinson Murray's 1951 book "The Scottish Himalayan Expedition.")

What calls to you is for you. Trust and believe. Become an 'Action Jackson.' Step off the curb. Move toward the other side, one step-at-a-time, and watch the magic of openings and opportunities as they unfold for you, too.

AFTER ALL, WHEN WAS THE LAST TIME YOU SAW
SOMEONE STANDING IN THE CENTER LANE FOR DAYS
AT A TIME? ☺

Since childhood, Lonnee Rey has been manifesting free trips, concert tickets, all sorts of crazy things, including winning the lottery. She is on a mission to reignite this power in others who have lost faith in their ability to create what they want in life. With more than 40 years invested in metaphysical, paranormal, "spiritual" and personal growth studies, Lonnee is a testament to the harnessing of the Source that lies within each of us.

Name It, Claim It, Make It So

Lonnee Rey works as a facilitator of dreams, making them come true for people who do not know how to write, but hope to become a published author someday.

Her transformational writing workshops, story coaching skills and use of paintbrush words help others take a chapter out of their lives and discover their message for the masses.

A 2023 BIBA Award-winning editor, "Best Indie Book of the Year," her most difficult and impactful project so far is this book, published August, 2024.

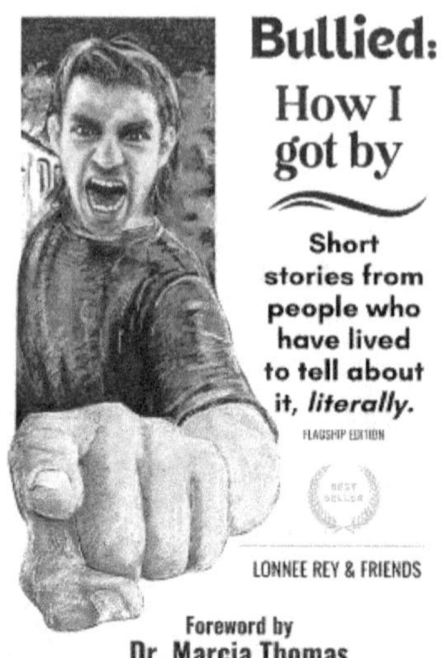

Please share this and help save someone's life. Available now on Goodreads and Amazon

Do you have a book in you? Get in touch with her to discuss your ideas today. Visit:

https://www.officialrattledawake.com/

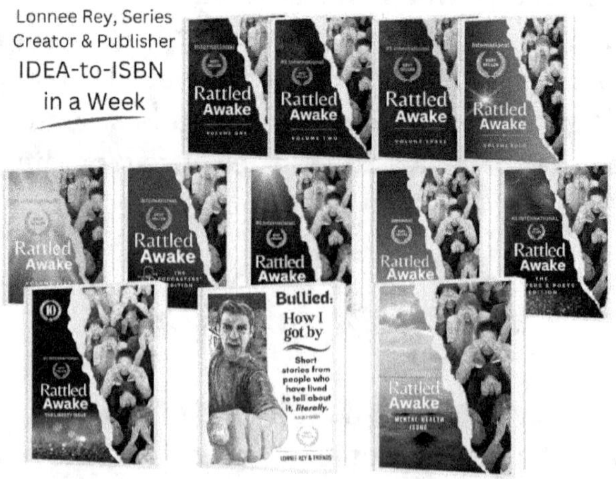

(anthologies, 2023-2024)

Lonnee has written two books that help with mental health in two different ways: releasing past issues with a parent, and choosing friends more wisely. Amazon links:

Life lessons   the 'Dumbass' book

Personal Freedom

SEAMUS CORRY ... SAVED BY AN ANGEL

One of the things that we Irish are really good for, apart from our natural charm and wit, is the art of storytelling. It runs through the very DNA we carry around with us. Would you like me to share a true story from my life experience ?

It was some years ago. I remember it clearly. It was a Sunday, the evening sun was shining in my car window. I was fucking done.

As I sat there in my car my life, as I knew it, was over.

I had just had the door closed on my first marriage. After seven years, my children left with their mum. My contact with them was now going to be limited and the pain was unbearable. My heart was broken, my spirit was broken, and I felt done.

I remember I was in my car, driving back to the emptiness

of my four walls when suddenly a very strong thought came to my mind. I could just speed my car up, close my eyes and all the pain would be at an end. The pain seemed to be all around me in that moment, I felt it in my head, my body, in every sinew. I was overwhelmed with pain.

I was in so much pain and had carried it for so long. The origins of the pain are beyond the reaches of this mere chapter. Suffice to say, trauma, if not processed and dealt with, builds up and comes out in all the unfortunate ways. I had been angry for a long time and in so much pain. I had let all my pain and trauma build up inside me.

Childhood trauma not dealt with, Catholic Church seminary trauma not dealt with, suicide of a close friend, not dealt with, being ostracised from my biological family, my community and my country not dealt with. Add to that the pain of loss, separation and emptiness I felt inside; all left to fester and come out in anger, paranoia, fear, frustration, resentment, and hurt.

I could go on and in a future book I probably will explain how all these events affected me. All you, the reader of this chapter, needs to know is this: Trauma, not dealt with, eats you up from the inside; it consumes everyone around you. It's like an uncontrollable dark vortex that tries to suck the life out of everyone in its wake, until the only option is to run from it and save yourself.

That's what my ex-wife did. We initially separated, I was to have limited, and eventually over time, no contact with my children. That was the final straw. I love my children; I have always loved my children. If they are reading this now, know that your dad loves you. I have always loved you and will love you to my last day on this earth. Not seeing them, holding them, being there for them, that is a pain I would not wish on my worst enemy. I decided I had enough of this pain.

So, I pushed my foot on the accelerator, saw the dial go from 50.... 60 ... .70 ... .80.... and closed my eyes momentarily. In that second between closing my eyes and hearing the car engine, a clear firm voice said, "**open your eyes**." I opened my eyes just in the nick of time as a car was approaching from the front. It narrowly missed me, my car swerved, went up on the grass and returned to the road.

Heavily breathing, I managed to stop the car, pull up on the side and cry uncontrollably for what seemed like an eternity. My mind was in bits, I felt I was completely and utterly broken with no pieces left. They had all been shattered and in that moment, I felt completely and totally out of control. I wanted to end my time on this planet, to complete my life cycle and ultimately, bring the pain I was carrying for so long to an end. I was suicidal and for the first time I felt really scared, frightened that I could conceivably kill myself. I wanted to end the pain, but did not want to die. I felt confusion; random thoughts going around my head. I had to find a way to feel safe, because the overwhelming pain I was feeling was making me ill.

I focused on what was directly in front of me. I was still in my car, The engine was still running, I wanted someone to help me understand what was happening to me. I felt lost, completely alone, afraid of myself, my thoughts, especially the ones where I could harm myself or kill myself in some way.

At that moment I decided I needed help. I needed medical intervention. I needed support, I needed someone to listen. I wiped my tears, blew my nose and focused on getting myself help.

I got my car on the road and within 15 minutes, I pulled into my local hospital's Accident and Emergency department determined to get help. I stood before the admitting receptionist and told her I needed to see a doctor as I thought I was in the middle of a full-blown breakdown with serious thoughts about injuring myself. I remember she was very kind, took some notes and advised me that there would be a wait as it was Sunday, and the department was very busy.

As I took a seat in the waiting area, I felt my body was so tired, I felt wrung out. Drained, exhausted, angry, sad... I felt soo sad. Something had died within me, and I was feeling the loss. I could do nothing now but wait. I was determined I needed help, and was finally going to get it.

I finally saw a doctor after a couple of hours of waiting. He took me into a cubicle and asked me to take a seat. I remember he asked me why I came to A and E. Without hesitation, I told him of the events earlier that evening and how I was feeling. I remember he listened, he saw me in bits, crying, as I told my story. I can only imagine how I appeared to him that evening.

After a few more questions, he asked if I would like to see the resident psychologist. I was open to all help; had nothing to lose. He completed some notes and asked me if I wanted to be admitted and undergo initial assessment so it could be determined as to the best treatment plan for me. I agreed. I was taken to the door of the psyche ward which was walking distance away from A and E.

It was a buzzer entry system. My charge pressed the button, identified themselves, advised the listener of a new referral and the door buzzed open. The door closed with a thud behind me, and I was taken to the waiting area which consisted of a row of chairs in a corridor, where I was asked to wait. I was told it could be some time until I saw someone, and they were really busy with other patients, I just had to wait.

It was so quiet, so still, the corridor was devoid of people. In the distance I could hear sounds of people moving, doors opening and shutting, but I remember it was peaceful. Occasionally, a nurse or doctor would pass by with a file or folder in hand. It was late and I continued to wait. I had no concept of time. Time seemed to suspend itself in this world I now found myself in.

After what seemed like an eternity, I suddenly became conscious of someone sitting down beside me. I must have looked a frightful state: no sleep, my eyes red and puffy with tears, just a general mess. The stranger spoke and asked if I was ok. I replied "not really." He then asked, "Why are you here ?" Wow what a question I thought, and I don't know if the lateness of the hour was a factor, my general disposition at that time, or feeling that I had nothing left to lose, but at that moment, I opened up and told the stranger why I felt the need to be sitting in chair on a corridor in a psych ward. It all came flowing out in one big blubbering mess.

The stranger just listened without interruption. It felt really cathartic to speak to someone else about how I was feeling. He just listened. When I was finished, he turned to me, looked me straight in the eye and said how lucky I was to have my freedom. If I was not already sitting down, I would have been knocked over when I heard this. What a really strange thing to say, I thought. He then went on to explain the reason for his comment.

He explained the reason why he was on the ward. He shared that he had been sectioned for 72 days to allow doctors, psychiatrists and psychologists to assess and understand what was going on with him. He said he was a danger to himself and others, that he did not fully understand his behaviour or why he acted the way he did. He said he agreed to be sectioned and as a result he had his freedom removed from him. While here, every decision had to be agreed, what he ate, the utensils he used, the medication he was on, who could visit, who he could see and more importantly, when he was ready to leave.

He then turned to me and said that right now I was in a pretty unique place. I still had the freedom to choose. I could stay and be subject to all the rules and regulations of the ward, have my freedom stripped from me and every decision dictated by others. My movements would be restricted; my life would be decided for me. Or, I could get up from where I was sitting, walk to the door and ask to be released back into my life. This choice was still mine and I was still free to make it. He went on to say that I had experienced a series of unfortunate events which led me to this point in my life. I could choose what I wanted to do next: stay here, or get on with living and sorting myself and my life out. The choice was still mine to make.

I thanked him for listening to me and for his words of guidance. He stood up from where we were sitting, headed back down the corridor and disappeared around a corner. I never saw him again. I didn't even know his name.

I felt a new strength. I felt lighter. I suddenly felt a little clearer in my head. I did not want to end my life any longer. Yes, I had to deal with all this pain I felt. Yes, I needed help and support. Yes, I was still free to make this decision. I did not need to be on the ward any longer. I no longer felt a danger to myself. I was determined from then on to fix what was broken inside and seek the help and support I needed. I know now I was visited by my guide. It was not the first time and would not be the last.

I have always felt close to my spirit guides and on occasion they have made a personal appearance. I am convinced this was one such meeting. I had been pulled back from the cliff edge and invited to see life from a different perspective.

I got up from where I was sitting, asked to speak to one of the admitting staff and asked to be released. After some convincing that I was not going to harm myself and that I no longer felt suicidal, they were happy for me to be released. The door opened, I walked through and heard the door shut behind me. I remember clearly that dawn was breaking. It was the start of a new day; I felt a little bit lighter in myself but also resolved to get the help I needed. I also needed sleep as I felt exhausted.

I got back in my car, turned the ignition and the engine roared back into life. I returned to my flat, put the kettle on, made myself a cup of coffee and looked out the window of my kitchen into my back garden. As I did so a little grey squirrel entered my garden to carry out his morning routine, searching, nibbling and burying its food. I watched it for ages and as I did so the smallest modicum of joy entered my heart. I, too, would search out the help I needed and be resolved in my quest to heal myself. I was also resolved to commit to seeing this little squirrel in my garden each morning and try to focus on what I needed to do each day to get well.

I did that each day; I became one with the wee squirrel in my garden. I became inquisitive about me; I began the search to find the real me behind the veneer. My journey took me to consultation with my GP, counselling for abuse I had suffered in my life, I found a meditation group locally and each week, sat and meditated. It was a result of being part of this group, I found peace, real peace for the first time in my life. I also found love, real love in the form of my soul mate, my bestest friend in all the world.

As I sit here and write now, the grey squirrel continues to visit my garden and reminds me on a daily basis that my recovery is a daily practice. The pain has subsided, I feel much happier. I acknowledge and accept my history fully, but my history no longer dictates my life. I am better, not bitter. I am grateful for so much in my life. I now try to share this within my work with others I come into contact with, and be a light for them in their darkness.

If you are reading this now and really struggling, reach

out and speak to someone, a friend, confidant, even a stranger who may just maybe offer the words that you need to hear.

I compare where I am now to sitting on a mountainous plateau. I can recognise the journey I have taken and appreciate the road I have been on, the steps I have taken and the climb I have ascended. I have slipped and fallen some times and got hurt. I have dusted myself off and continue on my recovery journey. I am not alone, I have a beautiful family, my soul mate walks with me, friends to support me and guides along the way to show me the direction I could take.

The journey remains, I am well, healthy, motivated, positive and grateful for every day I wake up happy and at peace.

I leave you with a reflection. I wrote this around the time of my recovery.

"New Direction"

Through the darkness, new light arises.
Of peace, light and hope, giving meaning to the experience behind us.

Propels us forward, slowly, stronger, wiser, deeper, closer, from captivity to the safety and security of love unconditionally.

Does this story resonate with you? Reach out to me and make contact. Here are my details:

Seamus Corry is on a global mission to change people's view of mental health and to support positive wellbeing. Married and living in Manchester in the UK, he is father, grandfather, wellbeing consultant and mental health instructor.

Chosen at a young age to become a Roman Catholic priest, he spent his early life achieving the goals of others. Ordained in 1994, he spent 15 months in service and saw first-hand the reality of the Church. He knew he could not stay. He resigned and left the priesthood and in so doing experienced the pain of rejection, immigration to a foreign country and loss of family and friends and a community who turned their back on him.

Rather than letting historical trauma ruin his life, he sought help and support through therapy and in so doing managed to transmute his pain into helping and supporting others over the past 29 years.

Today, Seamus is a successful founder, wellbeing consultant, podcaster and mental health instructor. He uses his experience to guide, help and support others who feel stuck in the mud of their life. With empathy, non-judgemental listening and pastoral mentoring walks with them for as long as they need to feel better and more resilient. linkedin.com/in/seamuscorry

https://seamuscorry.co.uk
Spotify
https://podcasters.spotify.com/pod/show/seamus-corry
You Tube
www.youtube.com/@SeamusCorryPyp

EILEEN BILD ... BE UNSTOPPABLE!

"Take me or heal me, I am not doing this anymore!" I yelled, looking up to the heavens, fist in the air. I am done, finished, tired of feeling sick and tired. It is a road well-traveled, the path well worn, time for a *change*. I have a dream and passion to be a light in the world. This was the catalyst for self-healing from Fibromyalgia and the beginning of a new chapter in my life building a legacy as a Breakthrough S.P.A.R.K. Coach, published author, writer, leader and trailblazer.

The Core Thinking Blueprint Method came through me in 2014. Since that time, I have worked with many clients to help them live better lives. One particular gentleman, who crashed and burned in his career in entertainment due to stress and pressure, was seeking a way to come back to balance. We met at a juncture in his life that soon became a pivotal point for change and transformation. In spite of his initial reluctance to release all his pain and anger, he has become my scholar student; deeply impacted by what I do with the Core Thinking Blueprint Method. His desire for lifelong learning and ease of dealing with life's challenges, but also celebrating successes, has enhanced his decision making, shifting from reaction to responding and understanding the value of the power of thoughts.

I love that I have become his mentor. Our rapport will continue because as life evolves, challenges continue, and he uses the tools and skills gathered over our decade together. He writes:

"Coach, I want to thank you for always being there for me. You have shaped me into a better man and helped me to become great. I appreciate you with all my heart, always. I hope to make you proud one day."

Once we got through the initial 90-day program, we continued to build, transform and evolve his emotional, mental and spiritual self as needed until we created a good solid foundation. As his confidant and mentor, I guided and continue to mentor him through the Core Thinking Blueprint post program process assisting him to be in the world with confidence, courage and clarity showing up in the authentic space. This is an "iron sharpens iron" strategy sharpening valuable tools and enhancing life skills for reaching higher levels of success.

Over time, he has built upon the years of personal and professional growth and for me, it has been incredible to see this angry person with a chip on his shoulder, with *the world is against me* thinking, to teaching and inspiring others. There was so much frustration, feelings of betrayal and judgment, and hopelessness. Family members accused him of being different - you know, the "black sheep" of the family. Because of that, he did not feel like he belonged in spite of attempts, much of his life, to please people who may never accept him for who he is.

Fantastically, he has truly walked with a spectacular personal power.

"This amazing course provides you with the skills to communicate effectively with confidence. These tools will help you build better relationships with other people in business, social networking, and career opportunities."

What does it take to change from one paradigm to another?

I had to find a way to live again and come back to my authentic self because I felt lost and out of balance from the Fibromyalgia. The dis-ease in my mind and body was robbing me from living my best life and I knew there was something waiting for me, a purpose yet to be discovered.

When I think back on my breakthrough and the following years of pivoting into who I have become, there comes a time to fully embrace one's gifts.You know how hindsight can show where we were and where we are now? I have learned so much about myself, how I show up in the world and what is important to me.

I have heard many times, "It is not possible to heal from Fibromyalgia." My experience defies these beliefs and if I can overcome something so devastating, anyone can find the will to heal and transform!

It is important to know that the way our thoughts get entangled in our mind, sometimes creating the "monkey mind," it can be difficult to break free. Re-engineering the brain to uplevel thinking and beliefs will release limiting thinking, sparking a new neural pathway, bringing hopefulness, gratitude and unwavering confidence.

There is a process of unlearning the conditioning and figuring out what really makes you tick. Do it not for others; do it for you. It is your life and your choice to live it the way that best fits your passions, visions and dreams.

My very first client for the Core Thinking Blueprint Program was in a tough career situation when we met. She was practically in tears not knowing how to leave her job unscathed. She was being bullied at work, threatened and was left feeling demoralized, weak and disempowered. Having been one of the top producers and an impressive background did not shield her from the destructive behaviors of the leaders of this company. Just 90 days into working together, she had this to say:

"Core Thinking Blueprint and Eileen Bild, WOW! What a life changing coaching experience of internal discovery and healing, strengthening and understanding. I am completely and genuinely blown away by the process of coaching with Eileen, but especially by the program she developed."

I know, firsthand, when I felt so beaten down, overwhelmed with the pain and intensity of the symptoms of dis-ease caused by Fibromyalgia, I almost gave up. But, deep within there was a voice that demanded "GET UP." Of course, I ignored it and it got a little louder while my symptoms got worse. One day, the stress point was more than I could handle, and the declaration came through to heal. I was exhausted, but then I was shown a new and healthier path.

With my own journey, one steppingstone at a time, I began to shed the old uncertainty of what my future held, replacing it with tenacity for building myself up to a level where I am unstoppable. This too is where my clients go: a path of clarity in decision making, communication and defining boundaries for others in how they want to be treated.

The spark that brings change is when the light bulb moment occurs. The point of no return, no going back because the shift is deep and real. My client, who experienced severe bullying, was SPARKED!

"It really opened my eyes to so many areas to the way that I think, the way that experiences in life have stopped me, so that my subconscious response was in many ways warning me. I was not getting to where I really wanted to go and into the higher levels of achievement in my life. What breakthroughs I experienced!"

Have you ever felt anger or a sense of loss for having spent years not honoring your core self - your true essence and becoming all that you can be? Do you have regrets of the past? Feel sad about what you have missed because you did not take the risk?

We all have unfinished business. We also know, from many mind-body studies and quantum physics, that old anger, grief, resentment and fear that is energetically entangled in the body-mind projects into our lives and can dictate our present and future. Being mindful in the moment is a present you can give yourself. The past is just a memory, the future is yet to be determined, so NOW is all you have.

I researched and dove headfirst into understanding the mind/body connection, getting my Masters in Transpersonal Psychology, not only for my healing but also for carving out my future.

Do you know how much is missed when not paying attention to what is right in front of you? It is life changing for yourself and others as you capture the nature of your state of being and truly listen for the messages coming into your life. Paying attention to my intuition and dropping out of my head into my heart center was mind blowing.

"I can't" becomes "I can!"
"It is not possible" becomes "Watch me, it is possible!"
"I am tired of difficult people" becomes "They will walk beside me or find another path!"

Amp up the voltage!!! Be unstoppable and see the possibility with unlimited opportunities. I know whatever I put my mind to, it will happen. There is no other option. We have two choices in life, say Yes or say No. The more you say YES to what feels good and what you know is your path, then the better your life experiences can become.

If not now, when? What are you waiting for?

I have learned the best compliment is when those you lead want to follow with respect for you and your leadership. When others feel heard, valued and understood, their mental state will be in creativity and innovation. The collaborative nature of teams can be productive giving you the freedom to spend more time in stewardship for the benefit of all.

There comes a time when the pull to do more, be more and fully embrace innate gifts is so great, it cannot be ignored. For me, my time is now, bringing opportunities to spark the next step for others with the Core Thinking Blueprint Program to a wider global audience.

Life continues to evolve and change, sometimes at rapid speed. It can feel like getting hit by a 2x4! But when you are aligned with your blueprint and inner compass, it is a different world that works with you and for you. Some call it magic; others may call it luck. Either way, you are the captain of your ship, guiding it with the assistance of the navigation tools and in the case of the Core Thinking Blueprint Method, you would be gaining new revelations for success. It is liberating to know you have someone for your mental well being and self-care for whom you can trust.

Are you ready to be unstoppable, too?

Eileen Bild self-healed (in three months) from Fibromyalgia, had an awakening that led to getting her Masters in Transpersonal Psychology, became a Reiki Master/Teacher, Breakthrough S.P.A.R.K. Coach and Founder of the Core Thinking Blueprint Method: 3 C's – Confidence, Courage, Clarity. She is the CEO, Ordinary to Extraordinary Life/OTEL Universe, and is on a mission to help others live their best lives.

She is also a Music Industry Executive and a two-time International Singer Songwriter Association USA Promoter of the Year finalist.

www.corethinkingblueprint.com
https://www.linkedin.com/in/eileenbild/

https://www.instagram.com/eileen.bild/
https://www.youtube.com/c/EileenBild
https://youtu.be/yeTDZRTif38
coach@eileenbild.com

ROBB PROFANCIK … LIVING THE 12 STEPS TOWARDS A BEAUTIFUL LIFE

GODDAMMIT!! LIFE SUCKS!!!!

This sounds familiar, right? Of course it does! I guarantee you have said it at least once in your life. I know I have and multiple times, too. There is a way to start getting to the root of what troubles you… what sends you on the brink of self-destruction. Please believe me when I say that you are not alone. I have been in the Darkness with that feeling of no escape…no hope.

To emerge from the Darkness was not an easy journey for me. I attempted many times until I finally and wholeheartedly decided that enough was enough. I was so sick and tired of being sick and tired.

I created these steps to help guide you on your path to a better, more fulfilling life. These steps have been influenced by another particular set of steps I used (and continue to use) to live a more beautiful life...the one I am living today. These are created to guide you and help you in reclaiming your wellbeing. I will mention the steps that influenced me at the end of this chapter.

I encourage you to take time to really read these steps. They may be beneficial to you, more than you realize. Whatever you are going through at this moment, always remember that you are not alone. There are others willing to help you. All you have to do first is reach out for help...that's the hardest part!

Living The 12 Steps Towards a Beautiful Life

IS IT TIME TO SURRENDER?

This is the first and crucial step in your journey to work on your wellbeing. Surrendering is NOT defeat. Surrendering in knowing you are at a debilitating crossroad in your life and you have nowhere else to go is the first action towards progress. It means you are ready to fully commit yourself to accept what is truly beating you down. To fully accept that whatever has its claws in you...whatever has made your life an unmanageable Hell!

CREATE/REVISIT AND STRENGTHEN YOUR BELIEF

Some of you reading this believe in God or have a God of your understanding – Higher Power. I know some do not and that is perfectly okay. To those that do not believe in God, you can have a belief that you can call your Higher Power. It is just a matter of being willing to believe in a Power greater than yourself. Nothing more is required and a foundation can begin there. This can be anything of your choosing: Nature, The Universe or whatever you are comfortable with. For those that believe in God or a Higher Power and those that have established one, now is the time to strengthen your belief to continue on your journey to wellbeing. Believe me when I say, having Spiritual guidance will definitely help in your breakthrough.

LET YOUR HIGHER POWER WORK FOR YOU

Now that we have established or reconnected with God (Higher Power), it's time to turn our will and our lives over to them. Yes, you heard me correctly, turning it over is a must. Why? You have seen that whatever your life is creating havoc for you, you cannot do this on self-will anymore. You realize you come up unsuccessful each time. I know I did! We all live by self-propulsion, where we are constantly in a collision with someone or something. Even with the good intentions that you believe to have, collisions are constants. Just let them go and have someone else take the wheel for a change. In this case it is God (Higher Power.)

LOOK DEEP WITHIN AND DIG

Are you ready to get to work?? This is where you take a good, hard look at yourself and see who and what you are. You will reveal the true causes of why you are where you are and what is blocking you from living the beautiful life you desperately yearn for. This is where you list every resentment and fear that you feel that are the cause of why your life is where it is. I mean list EVERYTHING that contributes to feeling mentally, physically and spiritually ill. Call it your grudge list. Everything that has affected you in any way: your confidence, your self-esteem, your ambitions or relationships. Do not hold back, because this will help you so much. One last thing before we move on, putting this down on paper will give you a better perspective of who you are, where you are and what needs to be worked on to continue on that path to a beautiful life...FREEDOM!

VERBALLY MAKE YOURSELF ACCOUNTABLE

Got your list all written out? COMPLETELY written out? Good!! Now go and tell someone! Yes, you heard me right! Go tell another human being and while you are at it, tell it to God (Higher Power.) This step right here makes you accountable. Not only are these resentments and fears now down on paper and out of your thoughts, they are spoken to another individual. You may be asking, "Who the hell do I reveal these inner secrets to?" Good question! This can be anyone you feel truly comfortable with and someone you can truly trust. If you have no one, then speak to a priest, pastor or any person of a religious affiliation. I do advise not using your immediate family. Also, never use a very close friend if this list may contain anything involving them. I know you will find someone you can talk to. Someone you can truly confide in, because this step is another MUST to move on in your healing journey.

GAIN CLARITY BY BEING PRESENT IN THE MOMENT

Once you have confided in the person you trust, telling them every possible resentment and fear, find a quiet and peaceful spot...and just be present in that particular moment. That moment where your mind is clear, open and free. Everything you just divulged to God (Higher Power) and to another individual should make you feel as if the weight of the world has just been lifted off your shoulders. Don't worry if you haven't. It does not always work that way for everyone. Just sit there and reflect in the calmness, *knowing* these resentments and fears, which have been caged for so long, have been released from your mind. Accept the peacefulness and relish in it. By damn, YOU deserve it! Whoever is reading this, I am so proud of you right now for allowing yourself to get to this point!

SPIRITUAL FORGIVENESS

This step can possibly go hand in hand with the previous one, if you choose to do so. After savoring this well-deserved moment, ask God (Higher Power) to remove flaws held onto for so long; to remove shortcomings that were in the way of our usefulness to ourselves and to others. Ask for strength to carry on your healing journey and to confront these, or new flaws, head on... and let them go. You deserve to be free and in doing so you will be.

LIST ALL THOSE WE HAVE WRONGED

The work isn't over yet. This step is the second part of freeing ourselves of the guilt, shame or anxiety we harbored in ourselves for way too long. What I need you to do, is make a thorough and complete list of everyone you have been harmful to. Everyone you have hurt in the past. Do not leave anyone out. If you do, it may be harmful to the healing you have worked so hard for up until now. A good list will include anything for as long as you can remember and what has not been forgiven already. I know this sounds ridiculous, as I thought so too, but you will see how beneficial it will be for you and for those you wrote on the list.

MAKE THE AMENDS

Once your list is complete, go out and make your necessary amends. Yes! Absolutely make the amends! When making amends, this is not an overnight thing. This can take days, months, and for some, even years. It is not how fast you get the amends done, it is your determination and willingness to. Every amendment will be different, you already know. A simple "I'm sorry" is not going to cut it. These amends are where you are letting each individual know you are sorry for what you have done by asking them what you can do as a resolution. Like the amends, the resolutions may vary. For example, an individual may want you to reimburse them for the wrong you committed. Another may ask for something entirely different. Whatever the solution is, you must be 110% committed to carry that out...ONLY if you are able to complete this task and it is not totally out of your control to do so. There are two other possibilities that may happen. One of them is where this individual accepts your amends fully without anything in return. Then there is the one individual who will adamantly refuse your amends and never wants to speak to you again. It will happen, so do not be surprised. If this is the case, just thank them and move on. Do not get discouraged. You attempted with every good intention, but cannot control their reaction. Say a quick prayer, if you are of faith. It can never hurt.

CONTINUE THE PROCESS DAILY

This is the step that will last a lifetime. Do not worry and get overwhelmed by this because it is only a continuation of the process you completed previously; just make it a lifetime habit. This is to keep your healing active and always growing from here on out. Keep tabs on yourself every day and if you mess up, admit it! Work on yourself going further. That way it is not tucked away in our mind to fester, as did the previous ones you just awesomely worked on! If we stay vigilant and also ask God (Higher Power) to remove these flaws as soon as they pop up, you will be golden. I know you can do this and have pure faith in you!!

MEDITATION AND PRAYER

This step should also become part of your daily routine to continue on the path of wellness. Do not worry, this one is easy if you truly commit to it sincerely. Meditate or pray at the end of each day reflecting on how the day progressed and how YOU were during the day. If you remember anything you do not like, then ask God (Higher Power) for forgiveness and the guidance to be a better person the next day. I know, I know, sometimes we do things in the heat of the moment, that we regret later. Perfectly fine! As the previous step states, just promptly admit you were wrong and ask for strength to not repeat this again. This usually prepares me for a decent good night's sleep. When we wake up, think about the day ahead and how you plan to conquer it. Will it be self-serving or filled with dishonesty? Of course not! This is where we ask God (Higher Power) to guide us towards a fulfilling and honest day. Remember the third step and how it was useless to do all this on self-will. Ask for strength and guidance to ROCK THE DAY!

PAY IT FORWARD YOUR NEWFOUND ENLIGHTENMENT

This step basically explains itself. Go out and share this spiritual, mental and emotional healing journey with others. Show them and explain to them what it has done for you. Not every individual will be receptive and that is okay. Give them details on your life and how it has helped you. Let them know it has strengthened your wellbeing and your life is so much better because of it. In some cases, you cannot help. They may not want your help, so never force it. Let them come to you later on, if they are interested. Wellness can never be forced. It has to be a choice of the person hurting. In whatever we do, from here on out, is to be done with kindness. Remember, an ounce of kindness can mean a ton to someone else!

Thank you so much for taking the time to read these 12 Steps towards a beautiful life. All of these steps have been influenced by The 12 Steps of Alcoholics Anonymous. If you would like to view them, they can be found on this website: https://www.aa.org/the-twelve-steps. The original 12 Steps have helped me so much in my time of need, in breaking through from the Darkness. The amount of people helped by these original 12 steps are profound! I thought about it and wanted to interpret these steps, in my own way, to create beneficial steps for everyday people, just like you! The choice is yours...what are you choosing?

Dear reader, I sincerely wish you a lifetime of Peace, Love and Happiness! You DESERVE IT!

Robb Profancik is on a mission to give others a sense of peace; by letting them know they are not alone in this life journey. Robb's main goal is to spread this through his stories of darkness to breakthrough, hope and happiness. He is a pillar to lean on when the weight of hopelessness is too heavy to bear and is constantly reminding others they are all miracles.

He is a machine assembler at Kiffer Industries, Inc., where he assembles and tests plasma cutting machines by day and he gives others hope, inspiration and encouragement with his amazing daily quotes he posts on LinkedIn by night.

His posts can be found right here on his LinkedIn profile:

www.linkedin.com/in/robb-profancik-□-3b5418156

In the 3+ years that Robb has been sober, he has co-authored in the International Best Seller Volume 5 of Rattled Awake and has 'stepped outside the box' to do things he otherwise wouldn't do. Robb is just living a wonderful and beautiful life!

Traumatic Brain Injury

CAROLYN S. SMITH … IT'S ALL IN MY HEAD

Hey, where are all the magnets? I am not talking about the ones that are clipped onto the items in stores, I mean the ones that are in doorways you walk through. You know, like the ones at the airport, sporting events, or concerts, those heavy duty ones. The ones that go off if you have any type of metal on your body. Most of us have seen what happens at the airport when one of the machines goes off because the elderly man has metal in his knee, or maybe his shoulder. You are pulled to the side and made to strip all the clothing you can and then the wand, the big thick yellow lined one comes out and goes over your body. Top to bottom and bottom to top. Geez, talk about invading your privacy. I never thought about them. I was blind to what others experienced when they got near a magnet detector.

Pre-January 2024, my life was so "normal" (whatever that

means), right? My day consisted of working, watching television, (crime shows) and walks with my husband and dogs. It was heaven, truly! I love my work! I work as a Billing Representative II, on medical claims that were denied by the insurance companies. Actually, at the moment, this is the past tense. I am on leave due to my brain shunt problems. This is/was my heaven! At this time I had a purpose that fed my soul. For me, medical billing is a field that I can completely immerse my soul in without any questions about how or what to do. That was the case.

Unfortunately, at the moment, I cannot walk
and chew gum at the same time.

In March of 2023, I began noticing headaches that seemed to come on and nothing I did would make them go away. I walked around like I was inside a huge bubble, and nothing was real. I couldn't break out of it, either. At one point I put a rubber band around my left wrist and would pull it to see if I could make myself wake up. Nothing ever worked and I didn't say anything to anyone. I just kept telling myself, "take another hill." Finally the day came when I became unfunctional. The pain in my head was so bad, I had to tell my husband. We ended up in the emergency room. Gawd that was awful, my blood pressure was 182/140, it was bad. When we got there one of the nurses said I could have a brain bleed. I was led to a small room where the nurses immediately set me up with an IV and heart monitors, remembering that now, I shudder, I hated that room. I was given some medication to bring down my blood pressure. Instantly, I began stuttering and telling my husband I was cold, and a nurse ran out of the room and called a code for a stroke alert.

I was so confused, I didn't know what was happening. I was wheeled to the CT Scan room. What I saw were five other people in front of me. They moved me to the front of the line and did the scan.

It was about five minutes after the scan that I saw a doctor, I can't remember his name, what I do remember is he was so nice to me. He said I didn't have a stroke. But he had ordered an MRI; was concerned something was going on inside my brain. Since they were going to do one of my head, I would have to be strapped down with absolutely no movement. Oh boy. It was late, my husband had to go home to take care of our dogs. I would have to face the MRI alone, without the thought that my husband would be there when I was wheeled back from the scan. More fear.

When they came to get me for the MRI, I remember being taken down several long corridors, turning left, turning right, and then going through double doors that only the person pushing the wheelchair could get through. Finally, we arrived at a location that was not fully lit. A tiny man sat at a desk. Sheer panic set in: I was in a place without anyone I knew. The tiny man scared me so badly. I just knew this was the end of me. The man came towards me and wheeled me into the MRI room, then asked if I needed help up on the table, I said no, and began to climb on the MRI table. I got up and then began to like back down as the man began securing the "hockey mask" that would hold me down. I was terrified, it was just him and I, no one else was there. He must have seen the fear and color drain from my face. He asked if I was okay and I said no and that I wanted to get up and out of there. He unfastened the "hockey mask" and helped me up and down into the wheelchair. He rolled me out into the area and called for one of the nurses to come and get me. I had refused to have at least one done by him. Then the sweetest nurse came and took me out of the long dark curvy hallways. On the way back to the ER room I began begging the nurse to let me go home that night with the promise that I would return first thing in the morning for an MRI. I promised to be a good patient and come back in the morning. She said no, they needed to get an MRI and they were going to give me something to help with the anxiety. One thing I did ask was that the nurse please stay with me while the MRI was being done. Remember, no one was there with me. My husband was at home, I didn't have my cell phone. I was completely alone with a hospital full of strangers. The nurse leaned down next to my right side and said, she would stay with me while the MRI was being performed.

By the time I got back from the MRI, they had moved me to another room. My head was hurting so bad I was trying to bury it in the hard plastic bed.There was no relief to be had, I was suffering like never before, *hell childbirth was easier than this horrific headache*. One nurse gave me something in my IV to help with my headache, she said it should help. My blood pressure was not cooperating and they said that was a concern for them. They were trying to keep me from having a stroke. I was admitted to the hospital that night. That was truly the beginning of all the changes. I was moved to a room on the cardiac floor to be continuously monitored. The next thing I knew I was in a room with a new nurse. My head hurting never relented. It was so bad and my blood pressure was still so high. The nurse gave me a headache cocktail. That's the last thing I remember. When I woke up a few hours later, my head was still in excruciating pain. Apparently there was a physician assistant from neurology that came by to see me. The only thing I remember from that visit is the insistence to see a neurologist as soon as possible. With my head buried under the covers I asked why? What would the reason be to see a neurologist? She would not give me a definitive answer, only direct me to a neurologist as soon as possible. I was *mad.* First of all, I hate not knowing what is going on with my body but then to have the physician's assistant skirt my question?! That pissed me off. It's my body and without explaining to me the reason for seeing a neurologist, right?! Each time a nurse came in to check on me they each said the same thing. This made no sense to me, if anything it only made me madder at the whole thing. Not one single medical professional would tell me the reason I needed to see another doctor. Hell, I was in a hospital with hundreds of doctors, and one of them could come see me about my head. Every time a nurse would come and check on me I would ask that one of their neurologists come and see me. Actually, a physician's assistant from a neurologist's office came and said the same thing. You have to be seen by a neurologist. That was the closest I ever got! I figured they were just not sure what the problem was and were referring me to someone who dealt with brain issues. One final blow to my ego: "You have to get a referral from your primary care physician as soon as possible!" This really pissed me off: telling me that I had to bring in someone else? What the hell was happening to me? Why won't they tell me? Later that day I was discharged with specific instructions to get to my primary care physician and a neurologist as soon as possible. Kind of like a game of monopoly, you can't pass go without paying whatever dues I was stacking up against me. At least, that's the way I felt.

I followed up with my primary care doctor and she referred me to a neurologist. I called and set up an appointment. The day of the appointment I was minutes away from canceling: stopped at a light, I thought "What the hell am I doing?" I should just turn around and go home. This sucks, not one person would tell me why I had to see a neurologist, not a single one! Hell, if they didn't know what the problem was, how could a neurologist know? This was stupid, absolutely stupid, I was missing time from work. That was a problem for me! I hate missing work, I have a routine, I have a life! Dammit! The light turned green and I turned into the complex for my appointment.

Once all the paperwork was done and they took me back, the neurologist was in the room within minutes of me sitting down. He began asking questions about the pain, what I was feeling and then said he wanted to see me walk. Once I came back to the room - I had to sit down. My freaking head hurt so bad I was pissed off once again.

He said "You have to see a neurosurgeon as soon as possible." My brain was hanging down 6 mm below my brain tonsils.

He lifted my hair and ran his hand along the lines where the neurosurgeon would cut and correct the problem. I asked him if it was serious, and he said I don't refer patients to a neurosurgeon just because. This has to be corrected. It would only get worse for me if I did nothing. You need to get in as soon as possible. He gave me the name of two different neurosurgeons. I selected one and off I went. Work would be impossible, hell I couldn't even hold my head up without excruciating pain. He also was concerned about my driving. He said once I got home there was to be no more driving. I drove myself home and cried all the way. I had a brain problem, my brain was hanging down 6 millimeters below the brain tonsils. What the hell did that mean?

The next step, another MRI, would tell the doctors if enough cerebrospinal fluid (CSF) was moving correctly in my brain. This was an MRI the neurosurgeon ordered and he made it perfectly clear that if things were good in my brain he would refer me back to the neurologist for treatment. Unfortunately, that was not the call I received: there was not enough (CSF) moving from my brain. This was something that had to be corrected.

Who was I? Why can't I do anything? I was so tired all the time and miserable. The pain in my head kept me in bed most days. If I did get up, I was sitting in a chair. I was so sick, I couldn't believe this was happening to me. I should have been working, at least that's what I told myself. Hell, I couldn't even get up without getting sick, work? *Really, Carolyn, don't you ever give up?* That was the message that went round in my head. I felt like I was losing everything I had worked so hard to build.

**Then it hit me... I was not any good
to anyone in this position.**

The initial hospital stay occurred at the end of July 2023, my visit with the neurologist occurred in the middle of August 2023.

Surgery was scheduled for September 6th and it meant I

would be in the hospital for a few days. The first 24-48 hours would be in ICU to make sure there would be no complications from the surgery. The surgery itself was about four and a half hours, a lifetime if you are a family member waiting for news. Me, the patient, I had no sense of time. What I do remember is waking up in the ICU in so much pain. I screamed that it hurt so bad and a nurse was at my side in seconds. I saw my daughter at the foot of my bed. That's when I got some medication in my IV and then I was out. I woke up several hours later, close to midnight. I felt so much better. I felt like the bubble around me had popped. My head hurt, but that was from the surgery. I could tell the difference immediately. The thick feeling of living in a bubble was gone. I was free!

The next few days in the hospital were spent going over what I could do and what I couldn't do. No bending over, no lifting, keep icing, no heat and call with any questions.

I was trying to find my purpose while healing. I ran across a posting of Oki Language Project Auction. The note stated they could utilize volunteers in Colorado. I thought this would be great! I mean it would help me with my computer skills, and my communication skills and it would help Elders! Bingo! I hit the jackpot! I was able to help some via computer! I remember sending an email asking a question about how to do something for the auction. However, what I got back had misspellings, and sentences that didn't make sense. I began questioning what was happening to me, again. Right around the same time I began to notice fluid building at the base of my neck. *This can't be good*, right? I mean, why isn't it moving? I called the neurosurgeons office and they said you have a pseudomeningocele tear.

All of this is normal, and it will heal on its own. Just give it some time. Meanwhile, my motor skills, my walking, talking, and just general malaise, set in. The back of my neck looked like I had testicles. It was getting bigger and the neurosurgeon kept saying all this was normal. This began in October 2023. By November 2023 I had 7cm of CSF in my brain. I found this out because of all the emergency room visits I had and the MRI's that were done.

The CSF was not draining properly as I found out that the surgeon had nicked a place in the base of my brain.

Per the doctor, normally these things heal; we just need to give it more time.

On December 5, 2023, the last time I saw the doctor he said he would do one more MRI, and see what, if anything, was going on in my head. Additionally, the final comment was "I do not want to place a shunt." The MRI was scheduled for 12.15.2023 and on 12.19.2023 I got a call from the doctors office stating I had to get surgery as soon as possible as there was close to 10 cm of CSF in my brain. The concern was that the pressure from the CSF would cause my neck to burst. If that happened, I would be gone.

On 01.03.2024, my life was changed forever. At that time, all I knew was I needed to understand what was happening. So, after the brain shunt was placed by the neurosurgeon, you have a general surgeon who has to run the tubing over the clavicle and into your abdomen. This allows the excess fluid to be drained into my stomach. If there was anything funny about this whole thing, it was that the neurosurgeon removed 6 cm of fluid before the brain shunt was placed. The tubing is a hard plastic that is pulled and runs through your abdominal area. It does not 'give' as far as moving it to a more comfortable position. The tubing is hard for a specific purpose. It is connected to the brain shunt and removes the excess CSF fluid from my brain so I do not get hydrocephalus. The brain shunt is constantly working. My particular brain shunt is controlled by a magnet setting. The initial setting was at a three, however this setting became too much for me. The brain shunt was draining too much. I didn't know this at the time. I only learned about this when we went to a different hospital for care. They did a CT Scan and said my ventricles were slit-like and I began to digress back to before the surgery. We did go see the neurosurgeon. His physician's assistant said, "You're good, nothing needs to be done." Then he blurted out, "Well, we'll just remove the shunt." I was mortified, and my husband wanted to hit the guy. I was sharing with him the symptoms of things that were happening to me and he blew me off. *If they remove the shunt, I die!* That was my cue to get up and leave.

In July of this year, I finally went to a different hospital to get checked out. I have been experiencing stabbing pain in my shunt, along with a wet feeling. The pain is so bad I have to lie down. In the ER within minutes the doctors came in and said your shunt is set too high, it's draining too much. We need to set it at a different level. It was at a three and now the doctors were going to move it to a six. They use what I can only describe as a cookie cutter to move the magnet in my brain. It does hurt as they are pushing and feeling their way around an object that is implanted in your brain.

My journey continues: I saw our new neurosurgeon and she said you need to rest your brain for a minimum of six months, *complete rest*. That was in July 2024. My new neurosurgeon told me that in the 30 plus years she has cared for brain shunt patients, she has never run across my problems. The brain shunt should be benign, and no pain should be present. However, that is not the case for me. It is a struggle every day for me. I am pretty much bedridden, with only a few exceptions. I don't go out, I don't get up to walk around, and I cannot drive. Most people don't understand, they try to tell me to get up, move around, get out, fresh air will do you good, *wrong*! The only time I even feel half decent is while I am in bed lying down.

My story doesn't end here. It is actually a daily struggle for me. I have doctor's appointments and when my blood pressure is too high I have to go to the emergency room for care. There is a concern that my brain shunt setting has changed. This can happen if I am around magnets, so my doctor said try to be aware of your surroundings. Try not to get too close to any magnets.

My life will never be what it was before the surgeries. I'm lucky if I can get through a day without any pain. So far, that hasn't happened. You want to know what hurts? Me. I'm working on my anger issues and acceptance of being a different person. *This totally sucks.*

One of my goals is to focus on the Oki Language Project. This allows me to use my skills set that I do have and rebuild what I lost. Every day is different, every minute is different. I hope you will remember to be gentle with folks such as myself. I am working hard to maintain what I know and still hold onto what I can. My happily ever after hasn't happened yet. I try to remember that sunrises and sunsets are huge for me! I want a new day every chance I get.

As long as I have breath in my body, I want to live fully without any regrets! So my story continues, there is not an end and for that, I am truly blessed.

Carolyn S. Smith is on a mission to bring as much awareness to our Elders as possible! Our Elders have so much knowledge that in some instances remain untapped. Interaction with our Elders remains one of Carolyn's top priorities. She is volunteering for the Oki Language Project, founded by Mr. Eugene BraveRock in 2020. Mr. BraveRock has kindly allowed Carolyn to volunteer her time in locating corporate sponsorships as well as donations.

Since Carolyn's Traumatic Brain Injury (TBI) in 2023 she has been sidelined with chronic shunt pain, unable to work or function in life's basic capacities. Her "new normal" means that simple tasks, like taking a walk, or sitting upright in bed, are nearly non-existent. She works hard to overcome her TBI, is co-author of the #1 Best-selling book, "Bullied: How I got by," and feels strongly about contributing to Rattled Awake book #11.

Carolyn S. (Bully Warrior Survivor) Smith | LinkedIn

OKI Language Project

Carolyn's Babies

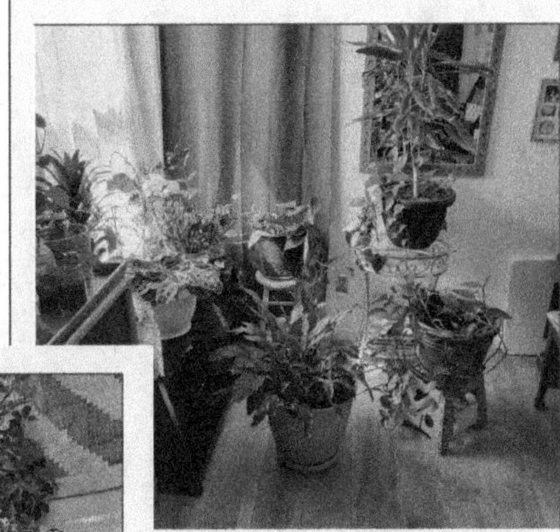

They bring me so much joy!

This was a baby plant gifted to me by a beloved elderly couple.

Changing the Future

DANTE' WADE ... A VISUALIZATION OF GRANDMAS' DREAMS

"**C**an I help you ?" I said to the customer as he stood at the window examining my face. He was a regular at our family restaurant in Newark, NJ so we had seen each other multiple times. This time was different though. My inquiry was accompanied by tears and a crack in my voice.

"Their grandmother just passed away", my father said as he prepared the order. Tears welled in his eyes but did not fall unlike mine.

My sister emerged to inform us that my moms morning commute of dropping my siblings off would be cut short due to the tragic news she'd just received. It's my understanding that my 13 year old brother called home to inform us as my mother was in the background crying profusely at the loss of her mommy.

It was not our first time experiencing loss but it never

gets easier. I recall the first time I had gotten a phone call about a death, unlike this situation where it was an elderly woman, it was a friend who had been murdered. Since that call I had gotten a call similar every year since. Some family, some friends, some illnesses, and some violence.

My grandmother's death was different though. It was like a final piece of the child in me had left. I wasn't as upset that she was gone but more so at how she had spent her last three years. My grandmother was one of the most independent people I'd known growing up. She owned her home which sheltered numerous family members over the years, hosted dinners, traveled throughout the east coast and was quick to get in her car and drive to wherever her heart desired. My first time on an airplane was with her when she took my sister and I to Disney World.

But everything changed when I got a call my senior year in college: she was found driving on the wrong side of the road. I immediately knew it was a sign of an unfortunate journey ahead. Soon after she would be moving in with us and our family would assume the role of caretaker.

My mom was able to get home and I called out of work as I felt my support would best be suited at home. Our family owned business had been a staple in the family and community overall since the 90s so naturally our home was going to be the meeting ground for the family. We finished out the day in the store and it was almost as if I was on autopilot, I don't remember anything about it except closing. It was after closing that I had to go pick my brother up from school. Dad was still cleaning the store, my sister was helping him and my mom had to make phone calls to inform the extended family. I picked my youngest brother up from school. He sat in the backseat looking out the window. I watched him in the rearview mirror as the silent tears turned into audible sobs. Next thing you know we were both in tears and I was letting him know that it's all going to be okay. Soon as I got home I just hugged him, seeing his pain hurt me and although I consoled him saying it'll be alright I really didn't know.

The first person I reached out to was my girlfriend Lici. At this time we had been together for three and a half years, two of which had been long distance but she was my best friend and her support always meant the world to me even if it was 1,812 miles away. Afterwards my sister and I immediately hit the group chat with our cousins. We had recently rekindled our relationship with them and had been spending a tremendous amount of time together. It was almost as if we knew we had to get close again so we can be unified for what was going to be our toughest collective moment in adulthood.

As the day went on more and more family members came over and soon we had a full house of aunts, uncles and cousins. Some were quiet and somber the entire time, some cracked jokes and tried to keep the mood light but almost all shed a tear in reminiscing on the beloved matriarch who was no longer there.

Later that night when everyone left I got on FaceTime with Lici to break down and decompress from the day's activities. In the midst of offering her condolences she just kept telling me how she wished she could be there.

Lic was in her second year of a four year contract with the United States Air Force, so getting the leave approved for your boyfriend's grandmother's funeral with less than a week's notice was not something she was able to do. I understand and she knew I did but it still didn't fill the void that was missing. We were about 30 days removed from getting back together after a two month break-up. Coming off of that break, our relationship had been stronger than ever but the distance was harder than ever because we just wanted to be near each other like every other relationship we knew.

When the dust settled, I said my goodbyes and love yous to Lic, the family was gone, and I just found myself sitting alone in my room unable to fall asleep. So many thoughts ran through my head. My grandmother was one of the most God-fearing and faith filled women I had ever met. She was in the front row of church every Sunday, was willing to pray with any and everyone who needed it (even if they didn't think they did) and even quoted scripture on her answering machine. Me and my cousins joked that upon her passing she would get to Heaven and talk Jesus' ear off about how much of a fan she was.

As big a fan as she was though, I thought to myself how that still didn't stop her from getting Alzheimer's. That still didn't stop her from losing her ability to take care of herself, drive her car or even remember her daughter's name. *I sat there in my frustration mad at God knowing that I wasn't raised to question him but the situation seemed like a fucked up trade off to me.* I couldn't wrap my head around how somebody who dedicated so much of their life to serving the Lord suffered a long slow process of mental deterioration before death. A certain bitterness came about me when I thought about it.

In the days leading up to the funeral my cousins, my sister and I spent every single day together. We would work our individual jobs and they would come over to my house afterwards to spend time together, laugh, cry and ponder on what the future would bring. The day of the funeral finally came and we all rolled together. It was a beautiful site to see all of Zora's grandchildren together entering the packed church to say our final goodbyes to our beloved grandmother.

The most impactful moment of the funeral though was watching my mother navigate that day. In a church that had pews filled with a sea of people dressed in black she chose to wear all white, signifying the new life and journey her mother would be embarking upon. A journey with no more pain, fear, medication or discomfort. She took the responsibility of being the caretaker for her mother and got to see the everyday struggles of what it's like to have a parent with Alzheimer's. For those that don't know, these struggles include persistent frustration, combativeness, wandering and confusion, to name a few. My mother took to the microphone and described the amazing woman that my grandmother was, the people she impacted and the love she had for her church and community.

I sat in the crowd reflecting on many things. One of them was my paternal grandmother's funeral. She, too, had passed away after a long battle with Alzheimer's, and for her, my family also served the role as caretaker during the height of those years. I couldn't help but wonder what the later years of life had in store for my other family members, parents or even myself. As these thoughts flowed I then took a step back and remembered the great things my grandmother was able to accomplish but mostly the faith that she had. I mentioned earlier the love she had for God and although I had felt bad about what she was going through, in the midst of her darkest and toughest battles if you asked her how she was doing she would proclaim that she is "Blessed by the Best", a phrase I still use till this day. I realized if she was fighting the battle of her life and could still believe that God's blessings were still upon her, how could I not when I have all my faculties.

The choir sang, my uncle preached an outstanding sermon and before I knew it myself, my cousins and siblings were tossing our roses into an open casket, and the day ended.

The day after a funeral is always strange. There's an awareness of the thought that "life really has to go on without them," yet, it does. The first time I lost someone was a former teammate, literally the morning of a track meet. I remember one of our rival highschool coaches who knew of our loss came to my team and told us something that I will never forget. "I know you all are hurting but I want you to know that the sun will rise again, tomorrow will come." At the time when he said it I was comforted, able to go compete and medal, but I didn't truly understand it until I had gotten older. Life does go on, yes the grief hurts and yes the grief will probably never not hurt, but as time goes by it will hurt less.

With the loss of my grandmother I told myself that I

may not know what will happen in the future but I have to operate in the utmost faith in the present that I can achieve whatever I want in this life and I have to go after it. In a discussion with my siblings and cousins after the funeral we made a promise to ourselves that we will be the ones to break generational trauma that has plagued our family, a commitment I fully intend to act out and hold them accountable for doing as well.

I can only speak of my experience, but from the time I was a child I knew I was destined for greatness. I simply never believed I was destined for normal. Over the years some have called it arrogance, conceit, overconfidence and a plethora of other labels, of course. It was my responsibility to make my late grandmothers proud of the young man they poured so much into. I was going to go after what I wanted in this life and live it with no regrets, unapologetically aiming to reach my full potential.

Two days after the funeral I met with my team for Reju (short for Rejuvenate), a healthtech start-up that I had been working on for the past year with some of my friends from Lincoln University. I attended there for my undergraduate years of college. We were in the process of launching our mobile application which was going to host a repository of mental health and wellness centered content for both Android and ios mobile phones. The motivation behind this company had been sparked from the mental health disparities I saw with my grandmothers, my family and in my own experience. I believe every problem has a solution and mental health issues are a major problem which needs to be addressed.

This is what motivated my team to get together and build a technology solution.

Starting a technology company sounds very glamorous when you present it to people, shit it probably looks glamorous as you read it right now, however it is anything but that. To break it down for you, imagine trying to ice skate, up a steep hill, in the rain. That *may* illustrate the difficulty of taking a company from the idea stage into an eight-figure valuation. Nevertheless I had faith in what we were building. That faith wasn't just in the concept as a business but in the fact that we were going to solve a major problem that affected over 17 million Americans on a yearly basis: depression.

We had finally gotten to launch day and I took a drive down to DC to meet with the rest of my team as we prepared for our event. I was nervous to share our concept with a room of 100+ people but with the support of my team members we crushed the event. We debriefed as a team after our launch and in the midst of telling the team how proud I was of them and the work we had been able to accomplish I took a moment of silence just to think of how I wish my grandmothers could see me now.

As we broke down for the event our CEO Aaron looked at me and said "Man I'm glad we got a good turn out, I heard about this virus called COVID that has a few people worried."

The coming days were followed with putting content into the app, meeting with potential clients and consistently testing for any bugs or fixes that our technology needed. This process was stressful at times because in the words of the great Erykah Badu "I'm an artist and I'm sensitive about my shit." Every negative piece of feedback or glitch or issue with the app brought stress upon me that, when looking back, was truly unnecessary. In any case, I found myself working full time while launching this product, helping my family pick up the pieces after our loss, and nurturing my long distance relationship.

The following month I got a call from work and we were informed that covid was spreading and my company made us go fully remote. The first thought that came to mind was "It's LIT, we're going to be home for a week or two, this virus is going to go away and life will get back to normal."

Well I'm sure if you are old enough to read this book you know that it actually wasn't "lit" and the virus only continued to spread in those weeks. After about a month of being home the yearning to be with Lic only continued to grow. I was working from home while all my friends and family were able to quarantine with their significant others. I was relegated to speaking to mine through the phone.

Well I had gotten tired of doing that and started letting some folks close to me know that I think I was going to take a trip to Texas to go see her for a weekend. The idea was met with some strong opposition as Texas was leading the nation in Covid cases. Understandably so, my folks whom I was living with at the time were leery about me getting on a plane going to Texas and coming back home due to the risk of getting and passing the virus along. The most bothersome conversation I had though was with one of my trusted confidants who

I affectionately called OG. OG was one of my coaches growing up who I kept in contact with and spoke to for wise counsel whenever I needed some guidance in the midst of life's curveballs. Me and OG related because we could have intellectual conversations, share business ideas and had great ambition for where our lives could go. Unfortunately OG suffered the loss of his wife in his late 30s and with her, his ambition to fight for the life he wanted. Nevertheless, he was still an amazing person and someone I trusted to tell anything to.

"OG I think ima head out to Texas, I'm working from home and I'd rather be with Lic than in Newark," I said.

"Youngin' you don't gotta leave Newark, your entire family and support system is there. Let this Covid shit go away then go see your lady," OG replied.

"Nah OG I know where my people are and they'll always be there, she is who I want to be with," I stated.

OG paused, took a deep breath and said, "Dante you on some bullshit, people out here dying from Covid and you trying to fly your silly ass across the country to a hotspot all for a girl."

I looked at him for a minute before replying, I guess I knew where he was coming from but my desire to be with the person I loved outweighed any fear I had.

"Well OG, being with her is where I want to be and what I want to do so regardless of what you say this is what I'm going to do."

There wasn't much conversation after that before we hung up the phone. I was heated.

Between the family, friends and even OG telling me not to go strictly out of fear, I felt stuck in a conundrum. I hopped in my car and got on Route 78 where I would often go for a drive to clear my head and multiple thoughts were ringing.

"Was I being foolish to get on a plane and go across the country?" I hit the gas: 80 miles per hour.

"Why does everyone have an opinion on what I'm trying to do?" 95 miles per hour.

"She's out there by herself and I'm over here playing the great debaters." 110 miles per hour.

"What's the point of me working remote and from home and I can't work wherever I want?" The speedometer was singing 120 miles per hour.

"Wtf is going on this year?! My grandmother dies, I'm struggling to get this company off the ground, the world appears to be burning and the one person my heart wants to be with the most is the furthest away from me," 130 miles per hour.

Eventually I slowed down and got home. It was a miracle that I hadn't been pulled over, hurt someone else or hurt myself, but I was in such emotional turmoil that for a split second I didn't care.

As I parked in the lot I sat and thought of what my next

move was going to be. Instead of politicking about the safety of my decision to travel back and forth, I decided that I was going to do something that I often had not done in the past. And that was to make a decision that I 100% wanted to make, not something that was going to appease my loved ones and respected elders. I knew in my gut was what I needed to do. That day I bought a one way ticket to Texas, with the time table of returning to Jersey "whenever the office opens back up."

As I sat in the airport waiting for my flight it was a ghost town. Convenience stores weren't open, vendor booths were nowhere to be seen and I had about five other people with me on my flight.

I spent that time thinking of both of my grandmothers. My maternal grandmother's faith rang in my head. During this time I was spending a lot of time praying and asking God to lay a path before me and I will walk it. I wasn't sure exactly what would happen but I knew my prayers would not be in vain. My gut was telling me I was doing the right thing and even though my decision wasn't popular at the moment it felt good. I heard a voice tell me that you're doing the right thing and in 5 years you'll look back at this distant memory and recognize all the blessings that came from it. See I can live with trying and failing but I cannot live with what if and I did not have a desire to live with the "what if" of not going to Texas.

My paternal grandmother's courage is something I often thought of during that time as well. She traveled from North Carolina to New Jersey as a single parent to establish a better life for herself and engulf herself in a new experience. That courage she displayed then rang true in my experiences with her as well. She was as spunky as she was loving and I never saw her back down from a challenge. She probably would've tried to box Shaquille O'Neal if he got smart with her. If I could talk to her right now I would thank her for her courage and strength to fight for herself, her family and what she thought was right. In many ways, she felt that she wasn't very accomplished, but to me she was a superhero, all 5'5 inches of her.

It's one thing to have courage and another to have faith, but when you are operating in both, there aren't many things that you cannot accomplish in this life. It took courage for me to leave everything I knew to begin building a life with Lic, yet, my foundation was having faith in the fact that I knew we could build a life together in the first place.

It took courage to decide I wanted to start my own company with limited resources and no investment dollars, but I had faith that mental health issues are not an unsolvable problem.

The hurdles in front of you can be scary but they're there to be jumped over. Some people follow the rhetoric that bad things happen, and that's just that, there's no lesson. When I hear anything remotely similar to that, my first thought is simply "You could keep that shit."

I know bad things happen but I also know of my own greatness and that God instilled this ambition for greatness in me for a reason. There isn't a tragedy, hurdle, obstacle that you could put in front of me that I won't learn from. I may fall and it may hurt but as long as I get my mind right I'm going to figure it out.

There have been plenty of times I've wanted to quit on my ambitions. There were times when I may not have gotten the job I wanted, lost my relationships, seen people give up on their dreams and consistently buried loved ones in numerous tragic ways. But I had to find a way to gain wisdom from my experiences because the weight of those obstacles was making me want to give up on what I knew I deserved. It's not just about what I may deserve though. Four years later I look back at this time and me and Lic are married with a beautiful daughter, Reju is still going and my family and friends recognize why I did what I did then.

My mission is not finished, though. People are still operating as though they cannot achieve their dreams, they've missed their window and have gotten comfortable carrying the weight of their problems. I mean this sincerely as I am writing to you in the midst of the most challenging year of my life, but there are tools and resources out there to help you overcome.

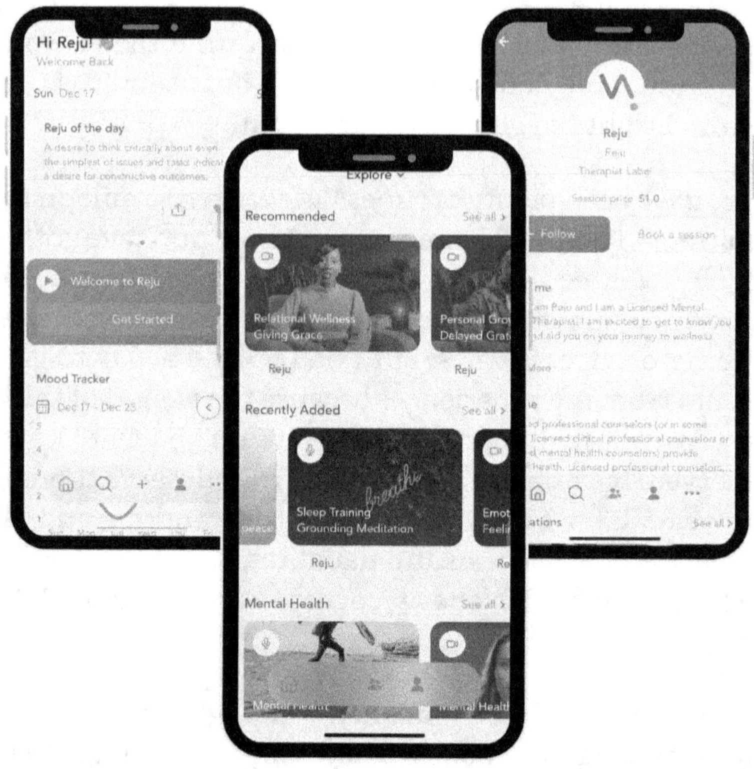

My mission is to make sure that everyone knows that with Reju.

So if you are reading this that means you obviously woke up this morning. If you woke up this morning, that means you have time to fill each day, and if you can fill each day, why not fill it with actions that will help you achieve the life you dream of ?

iOS: https://apps.apple.com/us/app/elevate-inspirational-living/id1four7fourfour6two8four7?ls=1
Android: https://play.google.com/store/apps/details?

id=com.app.elevates

Dante' Wade is on a mission to inspire community development, promote mental health, and help people live better lives. A New Jersey native from Newark, Dante has over seven years of experience in business development and operations. After earning his degree in Business Management from Lincoln University of Pennsylvania in 2017, he quickly established himself as a leader with a passion for innovation and community service.

Dante' has held key roles, including National Director at a large non-profit and Assistant Vice President in higher education. His expertise lies in building corporate partnerships within the workforce development sector. As the Co-Founder and Chief Operating Officer of Reju, a mental health and holistic wellness mobile app, Dante' drives operations, strategic partnerships, and team alignment to empower users to achieve physical, mental, and emotional well-being. Through his work, he remains dedicated to positively impacting lives.

https://www.linkedin.com/in/dante-wade-963622143/

https://www.instagram.com/_kampaign7?
igsh=N2s4dTc4Ynp4MTBj&utm_source=qr

or @_kampaign7

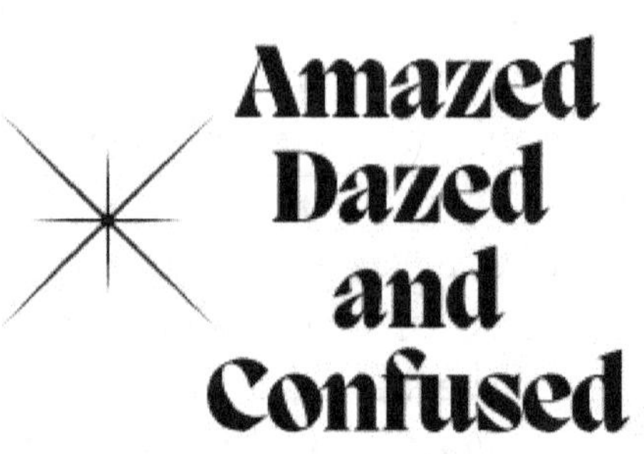

Amazed Dazed and Confused

HATTIE NUFF ... DECEPTIVE COMRADES

An open letter to posers and bullshit artists:

You walk away, sneering, laughing and scot-free. In the wake of your callous, cold and cruel behavior, I am left a shell of a person. The swift kicks you so easily 'administered' have left me breathless with pain, shock and disappointment so huge the only way I see out of it is to disappear, as if I am the one to blame for your abhorrent behavior. You have no idea – or maybe you do – that in the wake of your selfish behavior, I am dog-paddling as fast as I can just to stay afloat, trying not to drown in a sea of sadness. You have broken my spirit. And still you laugh, tossing more fuel on the fire, an arsonist of the soul. In your twisted brain, you feel justified in burning down the house. Oh, the presentation you make just shines, doesn't it? But you are a thief, stealing all you can then crying "wolf."

You are not the only one who has taken advantage of my kindness, espoused empty promises, failed to follow through, and simply walked away as if nothing happened. You are not the only one who promised to be there but never returned my call for help; never came through like you said you would do. No, you are not the only one to use me – but you are the last one…the straw that broke the camel's back. You are the reason for a river of tears, and deep gouges in my heart – the one you drove over, backed-up and did it again…just for good measure. Your claims of friendship and support, mere lies told with a smiling face and feigned compassion. At best, you are a frenemie.

You, my deceptive comrade, have shown your true colors. Your apathy hurts most of all. Your immature choices, malicious gossip, and bullying have taken their toll. Little do you realize the damage done – nor do you care, apparently.

There is a name for people like you:
Narcissistic sociopath.

A narcissistic sociopath, also known as Narcopath, is one of the most dangerous and psychologically disturbed people. They display both narcissistic and antisocial personality traits, which is the worst combination of personality disorders someone can ever have. You fit the bill, so let us count the ways. Everyone should know how to spot the narcissistic sociopath in the room:

1. They are very charming but pathological liars – they charm, disarm and do a lot of harm. The song, "Smiling

Faces" tops their playlist.

2. Narcissistic sociopaths live in their made-up reality – thick as a brick; can't understand normal things; refuse to see anything but their made-up "reality" through a deeply-filtered and short-sighted lens.

3. They are obsessed with power and control – they will stop at nothing to manipulate and maneuver people like pawns on their chessboard.

4. Narcissistic sociopaths' morals are nonexistent – ruthless but also 'gutless wonders' whose sense of right and wrong is questionable, at best. Their word means nothing, count on it.

5. They have limited access to emotions – must be some great meds, or is it merely a TinMan in disguise?

6. They easily discard people –A noticeable lack of manners, consideration or concern for anyone but themselves, they swiftly shift to new camps and enroll, engage (or bullshit) a new slew of clueless minions.

7. They are very aggressive when threatened – bullying-up to the bar, they serve-up lower-than-low blows to seal the fate of their target, feeling no remorse but rather justified beating their opponents, whether real or imagined.

8. They feed off negative energy – Queen Bees & Drama Queens thrive off the hive mind; they place themselves as the center of attention while being the linchpins of maliciousness.

9. They do not feel any remorse when hurting others – take note of their deflections and denials. Try not to get wet from their back-paddling.

10. Narcissistic sociopaths are sadists – they get pleasure from inflicting pain on others

You are not entirely to blame for prompting suicidal ideations. No, it wasn't just you who let me down. It's the many before you…seems we have an epidemic of classless bullshit artists, con men, "Wizard of Oz" types hiding behind walls, smoke-and-mirrors.

Sadly, even more than hurting me at work, you left a hole in the whole team. You let everyone down and thought nothing of it. Then, you gathered others around to support your notions of injustice and excuses. Nice job.

The collateral impact of your behavior left indelible footprints on everyone's reality. Who in the hell do you think you are, aside from a vain and self-centered escape artist?

If you think it's ok to corral your friends and wage a war against another to justify your insanity, think again. If you wonder why people commit suicide, look in the mirror. The sheer and utter destruction of another person, which you so gleefully do, marks the beginning of the end for those who have suffered at the hands of others who behaved *exactly* like you, and yours, do.

Eventually, even a willow tree will break.

Will you congratulate each other for eliminating the

competition you ruthless bastards? Are you proud of the ways you have banded together to support your cliques of unconscious, half-lidded malcontents?

Here's a newsflash: you are not entitled, gifted or owed special treatment. I see you out there, shaking your rattle like a spoiled child, boo-hoo'g about how you were done wrong. No, you are not who you think you are, unless, of course, this open letter hits a little too close to home, and you know exactly who you are.

Are you proud of yourself? Do you delight in fooling people into thinking you give a rat's ass about mental health, being "heart-centered" or community-first? What a hypocrite you are! The fact remains you destroy others' sense of well-being and business for sport. You and your cronies, seeing yourselves as superior to everyone else, are nothing but hollow, soulless beings wielding swords of flowery words and baseless condemnation.

Your attempts to subjugate others with contracts that bind them are frivolous pieces of paper you hide behind. Your titles, claims to fame, and purported service to all will no longer shield you from the ones awake enough to see right through you.

If a man does not have his word, he has nothing. Are you able to do that math, yet? No? No surprise, baby. Keep on shaking your rattle. Your once-covert actions are being brought to light. We hear you loud-and-clear. Eventually, that bleating voice of yours will go hoarse and the throngs who support your vindictive actions will run...*if* they are smart.

For those with eyes to see, it is clear who you all truly

are, drama queens, bullies and con artists, alike. The next time you reposition that tiara of yours, and think yourself all-powerful, all-knowing, think again. That crown is slipping and will soon be shackles around your ankles. Have a nice trip, deceptive comrade.

You may have pushed me cliff's edge, but what you didn't count on was me sprouting wings.

Hattie Nuff is an investigative reporter whose examinations on the recent shifts in human behavior are soon to be published in an expose-style novel "Nuff Said: Essays on the Erosion of Etiquette." Look for it in Spring, 2025. You can reach Hattie here: hattienuff2@gmail.com

They Need Us

P. TODD MORGAN … OUR CUBS

Searching the web today, and not sure how I ended up at an article titled, "Boy Scouts, US Supreme Court 2.46 billion dollar settlement."

As I read the article, I discovered 82,000 men have joined in this class action lawsuit as victims of sexual abuse, and will share in the settlement. Initially, we celebrate this as a success, because we live in a world where everything is monetized, and money solves the problem. However, in actuality, it does nothing to solve the problem, and creates deeper psychopathy.

I'm reminded of Dr. Max Gerson, whom Albert Einstein called one of the greatest physicians ever, and founder of the famous Gerson therapy, resulting in the highest cancer cure rate in the world. Dr. Gerson famously said "there is only one disease, therefore there is one cure and what cures one disease cures all disease."

To find the cure or the remedy, one must first determine

the cause; in the case of a physical disease, it is deficiency. In a mental illness i.e. disease, the deficiency is defined as disassociation. This is where we get the mental illness known as dissociative identity disorder, formally known as multiple personality disorder.

In the physical illness or, i.e. disease, the body is out of balance for a lack of nutrients. These nutrients come from the earth. Earth is an anagram for heart, and the Earth is our mother.

With a mental illness, the mind is out of balance due to disassociation from our Divine feminine mother; as the Earth is her anthropose, her physical being.

In nature, we watch a mother bear: the one thing you never want to do is come in between her and her cubs. We've all watched what happens when a male bear starts sniffing around, and that mother bear will unload a violent fury against that male bear to protect her cubs.

It's ironic that the animal coming to attack her cubs isn't outside predators, it's actually grown male bears. In the case of the Boy Scouts, they start out as Cub Scouts, separate those cubs from the protection of their mother, i.e. the Divine, feminine, and then adult males, predators, come for them.

Children, especially young boys, have inherent trust or expectation that their mother will protect them, so, when these young boys are sexually violated or abused, it creates another level of disassociation or distrust that a young male will have for the female.

This disassociation starts moments after the child is born: it is instantly taken away from his mother, it is in injected, with a hypodermic needle full of neurotoxins, and, if the child survives that, and it's a male child, it is in subject to sexual assault.

This sexual assault is when a female nurse will strap the child down and stimulate the penis to force blood into it then razor cut the young boy's foreskin off. This foreskin is the most sensitive part of the boy's body and the pain is horrific, so this child is traumatized right after it is born and has his first sexual experience resulting in genital mutilation. And we wonder why we have mental health issues.

Growing up, a child will spend 90% of its time with its mother. She provides that child with her milk, her nurturing care, her love, and her protection as the father, the provider is working, leaving the child in her care.

Therefore, we had to ask what is causing this mental illness, this psychopathy. We see in religions that in Gnosticism, "Sofia," who is wisdom, becomes the mother Earth. However, in the Abrahamic patriotic religion, they refer to earth as the father land Adamas.

Now we have the young male growing up with distrust for the female through the experience of sexual abuse. The male forms a trauma bond with the perpetrators, and then in many cases, continues the behavior.

Now this young male grows up to an adult and has

children and the abuse will be on the daughter: she will develop her disassociation for the male. The cycle continues in this endless loop of trauma based control.

In the original creation story of the gnostics, the heavenly realm is known as the Playroma where the highest creator or source energy is known as the monad. Source energy had its first emanation, Barbelo, capable of parthenogenesis. In other words, she doesn't need a man. However, she does nothing apart from him. Everything they do is together in balance. She asked for wisdom, she got it; she asked for a child, and they produced a child. That child is us, and in that realm, we are known as Aeons.

One of the Aeons is Sophia, which is the Greek word for wisdom. Sofia decides to have a child without the approval of her father and her consort. This imbalance resulted in the creation of the entity we call the Demiurge or Yaldabaoth.

The Demiurge is a word that means craftsman, or the creator of the lower realm that we live in. This demiurge goes on to create his own entities, known as the Archons. The demiurge, and these Archons, are psychopaths; we know them today as Masons. These entities have a hatred for the Divine feminine, and we now find ourselves embroiled in their battle against her.

Almost all world religions are based upon the worship of this entity, called the demiurge. In the Abrahamic faiths you want to see him as Yahweh, or Jehovah; he is also the God that the Masons worship as the grand architect. These are all patriarchal worship, and the enemy of our divine feminine mother.

In the gnostic creation story, the demiurge, a.k.a. Yaldabaoth, decides to copy the higher realm and create his own realm. He and the other Archons fashion a human host body out of the mud, affectionately known as mud man. But there is a problem: there is no divine source in him. The higher Aeons decide to correct the problem, teach Yaldabaoth a lesson, and Barbelo releases just a drop of her essence into Adam through Zoe, whom we know as Eve.

This infuriates Yaldabaoth because the entity he desired to create as a slave now has power over him. In his ignorance, he has kicked his own ass. He then throws them both out of the garden, but not before the Archons assault Eve.

This horrible assault and rape, impregnates Eve, with two children, Cain and Abel, and we know the story from there. These are the children of the demiurge, and they propagate through that bloodline in, or what we know as, psychopathic bloodlines.

These are the secret societies, the oligarchs, the rulers of this realm, and they derive their power from us, and the abuse of our children.

These Archons are male, but are also androgynous, having both sex organs. Their goal is to create a human that is also androgynous and capable of parthenogenesis. This is their ultimate goal. This is also why there is an attack on human sexuality and the transgender movement.

Again, you will always hear me say the root cause of all of this is disassociation of our Divine feminine mother. Everything in this patriarchal world is an attack on her and to me this is the root cause of all or the basis for all mental illness.

Now that we know the root cause or the source of this psychopathy, being that our world is run by these entities, we must now provide a remedy. Remedy begins with gnosis, or, knowledge. From gnosis we get the word gnostics.

Knowledge of who they are, how they operate, and where they get their power from: us, the host to these parasites. First thing we do is cut them off from all access to them from our children.

We then stop feeding them with our energy; we renounce and denounce all allegiances, all worship, and praise to any male deity, and reclaim our sovereignty, our power, our inheritance, and our access to direct source energy in the pleroma.

We don't oppose, we expose who they are, and we demand justice for the crimes they committed against mankind. It is most important to know there is no one coming to save us, no Messiah. This is up to us.

These false religions want us to believe that the end has already been determined, it has not. It wants us to believe that a Savior is going to come and fix all of our problems; there is no savior coming. It wants us to sit and do nothing, while it continues to grow stronger and more powerful. We cannot allow this to happen any longer.

We did not come into this world to continue building this prison, slave, soul harvesting realm. I believe we are here to destroy it and tear it down. Is it time for a new renaissance, a New Era?

Salvationism is an operating program in the mind, it is malware, and we must be like a computer virus: injected into it, to destroy it.

You cannot fight and win against the same enemy that you are worshiping. The God of the Bible, is not our creator, he is a copycat, and an imposter, creating a copycat realm of our original home.

As Men we have one responsibility, one purpose, and that is to love, honor, cherish and protect and provide for our wives, our daughters, our mothers, and to train our young boys to do the same. The rise of the matriarchal man has begun.

In the case of the Boy Scouts, we recognize this is actually just a cover organization, founded by the Masons, for predators to groom young boys. Over 82,000 men have attested to this, so far. The recent Supreme Court ruling brings this to light and is gnosis, the beginning of knowledge. These are our cubs. Now, WE must put an end to this organized predatorial "club" - we are the One we seek.

P. Todd Morgan, CHA, is a native Floridian born and raised in Daytona Beach and is a third generation hotel builder, developer and operator. Todd is owner and operator of the Daytona gym, a private MMA school. He is a two-time ultra-heavy weight freestyle grappling and Brazilian jiu-jitsu champion. Todd is also a researcher and activist, exposing what he calls as the evils of Abrahamic, masonic, Christian Salvationism, and how to return to our divine feminine creator. You can find Todd on his channels "Big Z" on the YouTube and Bitchute platforms.

HAWK'S INTRODUCTION

*I am offended when people
say "People are people. They
can't and won't change."*

I have spent 22 years in social work, seeing change happen every freaking day at work. I have seen kids and youth thrive when they have been given the environment where they CAN grow.

But ... and here is the big BUT: Do you provide that environment for yourself?

In the West, we are so concerned with giving children a safe environment, we are turning them into animals in a zoo. At the same time, we spend so much time on our cellphones, staring into the glamor of Instagram or the joviality of Facebook, that we forget to look into their eyes. And ... create attachment disorders galore.

In some countries, parents are so concerned with academic prowess and "getting into the right school" that they forget to see their children. CNN reported that in 2020, suicides among Japanese children aged 6 (!) to 18 hit a record of 415.

That same dreary statistic can be seen globally. An increasing number of people are choosing to end their lives.

Every 40 seconds, someone chooses to die; 800,000 in 2019, A number that is probably too low, as suicide carries a stigma which leads to under-reporting.

And what do we do? How do we fix this?

I know what I would do. I would infuse a healthy dose of happiness into the lives of those who have lost their zest for life.

But ... that sounds really abstract. You can't buy a pill of happiness at the local pharmacy. Though the SSRI's and other antidepressants are called "happy pills" in Norwegian, the truth is that since antidepressants entered the global market, everything has gone to Hell.

So ... how does one inject someone with a healthy antidote of love?

You see the person. You see that we are all uniquely formed, uniquely created. You do a thorough examination, and you ask, "What is this person's raison d'etre?"

Some people thrive on following protocol. Like bees, they need a clear-cut path and clear-cut objectives.

Others need creativity and liberty. They want to explore, explore and explore, until there are no borders left.

Some of us can't live without dogs. Others need a cat to purr on their lap. Others again would rather not have anything to do with animals, except neatly laid out on their plate.

Happiness may seem abstract. Ecstasy, likewise.

But please ... dear reader. I will use an example from

the Bible, but you find similar scripture in all the major religions:

We came here to love. We came here to care. We came here to do unto our neighbor.

When the world is going the way it is, when life becomes such a major drag that more than 1% choose to leave - isn't that an indication that something is wrong? That we need to do something different?

Perhaps ... to regain the joy we had as children?

There is a question I suggest you ask your therapist, if s/he wants you to pop a drug: "Have you tried it yourself?"

If the answer is "no" ask "Why?" Life is a journey with its ups- and downs. Depression, psychosis, anxiety - it is all a spectrum that we touch.

My life as a monk may not be yours. But having left psychiatry behind has given me deep insights into myself and others. And a multitude of beautiful meetings with people who are working to change the world for the better.

-      I had to find a way to heal, because psychiatry was making me sick.

-      I had to find a way to heal others, because psychiatry is making the world sick.

-      I had to find a way to dissolve fear, because the Man uses fear to control us.

-    I had to find a way to survive on little, because that was what I had.

-       I had to accept the certainty of death to survive.

I want to invite you to ask yourself some questions. Please read them out loud, and answer:

"How do I want my family and friends to remember me when I have gone over the rainbow bridge?"

"What is the smallest change I can make today to improve my life tomorrow?"

"Is there anybody whom I can help, in order to help myself?"

In this book, people from all walks of life present their perspectives. Some of the chapters are easy reads, others may trigger you. Rattle you awake. Make you angry, sad, or happy.

They all come from love.

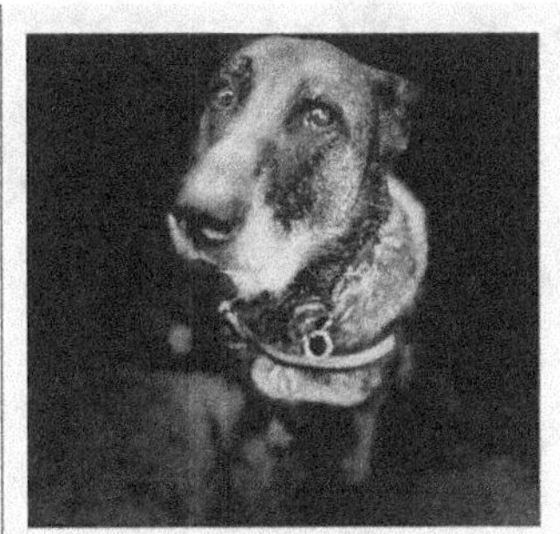

Trollheads Nessi
I see my love reflected in your eyes

Hawk's trusted companion...

Psychiatry Pills and Policy

HAAKON RIAN MANCIENT
UELAND ... LOVE – THE ANTIDOTE

A simple three step
process to happiness

Grasping cellphones like children with pacifiers, hordes of zombified people wander aimlessly in a mad world. Akin to a psych-ward where the patients least capable have been left in charge, Mother Earth stumbles through the universe.

Overmedicated, fed by emotions filtered through a screen, polarised by greed and consumerism, we chase the something that will bring meaning to our lives. The next pill or therapy that will help us feel good.

Are we living in 1984? Is this a possible future, or is it the present? And ... most importantly – how can we fix it?

When psychiatric drugs first appeared in the late 1950s, they were considered a godsend. Chlorpromazine was originally developed as an anaesthetic, but showed that it could calm down those who were called "psychotic."

Today, this has grown into a jungle of different varieties of psychotropic drugs, which are categorised into major classes such as antidepressants, antipsychotics, mood stabilisers, anti-anxiety agents, and stimulants.

In Iceland, which was ranked as the second happiest country in the world in 2020, 52% of the population use antidepressants. Are they genuinely happy, or merely sedated?

The term "psychiatry" was first coined by the German physician Johann Christian Reil in 1808. Mental disorders were considered a disorder of the mind rather than the body or soul. If you go to therapy, dear reader, please ask your psychiatrist to define "mind." What is it that they treat?

Diagnoses are often subjective, raising questions about the scientific basis of psychiatry. Based on the observance and interpretation of behavior, and created by committees. Which raises another question: "Does psychiatry adhere to the rigorous standards of the scientific method?" A person may show the signs of clinical depression, when they actually are deep in meditation or writing a symphony.

The standard treatment of mental "illness" in the West is to numb emotions with pills. My psychologist mother called them chemical lobotomy.

"Follow the money" is often used to identify the root of a problem. In 2023, the global psychotropic drugs market was valued at approximately $21.3 billion and was expected to grow to $28.9 billion by 2033, with a compound annual growth rate of 3.1%.

My first encounter with psychotropic drugs was back in 1994. I had read "Listening to Prozac," by Peter D. Kramer, and was enraptured by the thought of a drug that could ease the strain of little money, lots of work, and a new baby. So, I started on Seroxat, an SSRI.

It drove me nuts. The raised serotonin levels played havoc with my system, and after a short while, I developed hypoglycemia. I remember taking the train to Oslo, and the bewildered eyes of my wife when I had to leave the train, one station early, to run to the nearest store to buy a chocolate.

I went cold turkey and experienced classic withdrawal symptoms. Lightning that ran through my head, feet running though I wasn't, and I was left with an acute feeling of emptiness. This spiral got me a bipolar diagnosis in 1997.

From 1997-2017, I gave psychiatry my trust. Following the advice of psychiatrists, I used all the five classes of psychotropics, with lithium the constant, before I gradually tapered in 2017. The rattled awake moment that instigated this happened in front of our bathroom mirror.

I had started a MindValley online course called WildFit. In the introduction, we were asked to take a picture of ourselves, bare upper body. I looked into my eyes, and a knowing came over me. I was dying. The drugs that were supposed to heal me were killing me.

Since I have been a therapist since 1983, and a healer since birth, I decided to fix myself.

It used to be that people were given compassionate

attention and care. Some people are out-of-tune with our world that they need full-time care. Others need attention in the form of talks. Some people find comfort in their priests or shamans. And some need medication to function.

Naturally, maltreatment also happened. People were lobotomized, given insulin- and electrical shock-treatment, and beaten. Psychiatry has a dark history. Let's not forget how it has been used by regimes to subjugate indigenous people, or others deemed of less worth.

My mother, clinical psychologist Reidun Ueland, wrote this: "Psychiatry still exists in its form and content solely due to closed doors and a hierarchical power monopoly. If ordinary people knew what goes on behind these closed doors, psychiatry with its

My mother, Psychologist Love Warrior Reidun Ueland

biological view of humanity and biological treatment methods would have long been abolished. Only those who follow the internal laws have access, and external scrutiny is largely prohibited. Relatives have no say, nor do they dare to, because they are well aware that there is no alternative for their relatives affected by psychosis. It is a well-known fact that psychiatry has, over the years, prevented alternatives. This is rather strange, considering that psychiatric history is full of experiments that have caused patients great suffering and many deaths."

My mother was not religious, yet she was one of the most

spiritual people I have met. She had a deep and abiding belief that if people were empowered, they could get a better life. Her speciality was giving hope to people who had been given the label "schizophrenic" or "psychotic."

Some of her patients visited her at home. I remember meeting one of them, S.

S. came running into my mother's home, a frenzied look at her face. I knew a little bit about her; she had been drugged with cocktails of psych-drugs for so long and in such huge dosages that they had affected her face and given her tardive dyskinesia – and left her non-verbal.

She looked at me, and then she started marching around in the living room, raising her legs up high. Then she stopped, to raise her arm in a greeting worthy of the SS.

I had to contemplate for a few minutes. Was she saying that I had a Hitler-vibe?

As luck would have it, I watched the news last evening about the rise of neo-Nazism in Eastern Europe.

"Did you watch the news yesterday?" I said. She turned towards me with an inquisitive look. "Did it scare you?"

She nodded. Tears came to her eyes. I understood!

The mental health of the world is miserable. If you look at important indicators, there is no hope. We are sheep walking towards a dark future. Suicide is on the rise, the most harrowing symptom of human pain, and 70% of suicides are men. An increasing number of people are given psychiatric labels, ranging from the simple ones ("depression," "anxiety") to the tough ones ("schizophrenia," "autism" and "bipolar".)

Do the labels hurt or help? A growing movement in the UK, instigated by a group of psychologists, is called the "Power Threat Meaning Framework." Rather than labelling people, they ask some essential questions:

1. How has Power influenced your life?
2. Which Threats have influenced you?
3. What Meaning do you give what happened to you?
4. What Threat responses do you use?
5. What are your strengths?
6. What is your history?

So, I am hopeful. As a community, we can fix this situation. It takes a village to raise a child. And right now, the world is our child.

When we were kids, we got attention. Without attention, an infant dies. A child can't survive without TLC and food. Then, life happens. Mum and dad start working. The child is put into kindergarten or gets a nanny, and trained caregivers shall compensate for the lack of parental love.

This is made worse by our attention-deficit way of life. There is always something happening online. A new post by an influencer on Instagram. A new trend on LinkedIn. A new cause to engage in. Or a new episode of your favourite TV-show.

Have you seen a parent going for a walk with their child, cellphone planted in their hand? The child uses all means at their disposal to invite their parent into their life. But, the addiction of the cellphone wins...

I like to think of the world as a living organism.

In a sentient being, there are differentiated and undifferentiated cells. Cells that have gotten a purpose, such as a neuron, and those that haven't: stem cells. And then we have cancer cells, which are on the spectrum. Undifferentiated cancer cells tend to be more aggressive and dangerous than differentiated ones.

This same metaphor also applies to organisations and systems. Christianity evolved from preaching about the judgmental God, to the loving God who accepted us unconditionally as presented by Christ. Neale Donald Walsch has been attributed with saying "Judgment has no place in a loving heart" which can be seen as a summary of his book, "Conversations with God."

Organized religion can become a cancer. Just like big pharma, a tool to subjugate and control people.

A year back, I lived in a cult called Linbu. I joined them because one of their core tenets was that psychology should be about evolution, not identifying abnormality.

This quote comes from their secret workbook, edited for clarity:

THE 4 STATES OF CONSCIOUSNESS

1st STATE: SLEEP

- ❖ is the lowest state of consciousness
- ❖ is a purely subjective and passive state
- ❖ all psychic functions work without any attention

2nd STATE: WAKING SLEEP

- ❖ the second state comes when man awakes
- ❖ in this state we work, talk, imagine ourselves

conscious, but in reality, it should be called "RELATIVE CONSCIOUSNESS."

❖ dreams still remain, only they become invisible, exactly as the stars and the moon become invisible in the glare of the sun.

❖ dreams can influence all our thoughts, feelings and actions.

❖ in waking sleep, we can only know relative truth.

❖ in the second state, man is less subjective.

❖ he distinguishes between "I" and "not-I."

❖ identification plays a big role in this state, and man is acted upon and manipulated by external forces, as a puppet is activated by the puppeteer.

❖ in this state inner unity is not present, no real will or permanent "I."

3rd STATE: SELF-CONSCIOUSNESS

❖ is a state in which man becomes objective towards himself. She can know the full truth about herself.

❖ periods of self-consciousness cannot come by themselves; they need wilful action.

❖ frequency and duration of these periods depend upon the control one has over oneself.

❖ acquiring this state requires long and hard work.

❖ the development of self-consciousness, permanent "I" unity and will can be found only in a community of souls. Men cannot find these methods by themselves.

4th STATE: OBJECTIVE CONSCIOUSNESS

❖ in this state, we know the full truth about everything. We can study things in themselves: the world as it is.

❖ even glimpses of objective consciousness can only come in the fully developed state of self-consciousness.

❖ in this state there is a consciousness of the cosmos, of the life and order of the universe.

Unfortunately, Linbu devolved. Greed became the primary driver for their work. So, I left them.

Have you heard of spiritual bypassing? Spirituality can offer comfort and a sense of connection to something greater. However, **spiritual bypassing occurs when individuals use these practices to escape or suppress reality** rather than face it. If someone says "my life has hurt me" –*just meditate on it, and it will be fine.* If someone hits you on one cheek, turn the other.

That was the wrong turn that the Linbu society took: believing that you haven't been given a free will, and with it, the possibility to change your life.

We see the same in the bio-psychiatric narrative. Though a psychiatrist may say "talk therapy is a beneficial adjunct, their focus is on tweaking your meds. As if a pill can fix your hurt emotions. This is stupidity to the n'th degree. You must make the changes you want to see in your world.

If a cancer cell appears in a body, it ramps up its defenses. To avoid metastasis, the immune system kicks into action to destroy the invader. A cancer cell does not care about the organism, only about itself. And cancers of the mind – when the Threats overwhelm your mission – aren't fixed by a pill.

When Jesus saw the moneylenders and merchants in the temple, he didn't turn the other cheek. "My house shall be called a house of prayer, but you make it a den of robbers" he called out, swinging his whip.

The world is our temple. We are the shepherds of our world. And it is time we, who have awakened to our task, take the responsibility. Be the warriors that bring change.

There are organisations who benefit from us being sick. Especially if the illness is chronic. It is a genius business idea: you tell someone that they have a chronic chemical imbalance, which means that they require lifelong medication. The meds come at a premium, and new medicines – so much more effective than the previous generation – will fix this. Do you believe that big pharma cares about your wellbeing? I call it *medical bypassing*.

I am a healer. And I am good at my job. If a client experiences no improvement in three interactions, it is time to find another healer.

This is the opposite strategy of big pharma. If the drugs don't work, increase the dosage. Or change to another drug.

In the Danish book "Noget i bør vide – Om uttrapning av Psykofarmaka" ("Something you should know – about tapering from psychofarmaka", Hanz Reiztzels Forlag

2024), psychologist and psychiatrist Anders Sørensen shows that the effect of the drugs is independent of dosage. Receptor saturation happens at a minimal dosage. This is the reason that when tapering off from drugs, going from a little to nothing is most challenging.

The hypothesis that people who have mental unrest have a chemical imbalance seems to be difficult to kill. Sørensen (ibid) writes "No correlation between a chemical imbalance and any psychiatric diagnosis has been shown."

People with low serotonin experience "depression." People with high levels of serotonin experience "depression."

Still, this is put forward as a truth. The foundation of biological psychiatry is flawed, but the treatment remains the same.

People are being hurt by the establishment. In the guise of "treatment," we are decreasing their timespan by 15-25 years. Now, please do not get me wrong. I am not telling you, if you are on psychotropics, to throw your drugs out the window. That would be like a heroin addict going cold turkey. It can kill.

You should taper gradually. If you wish. Do it along with a professional and take your time. In this Newsweek-article, Sørensen offers advice on how to do it: https://reidunueland.com/kickdrugs/

By the way: I know that there are psychiatrists who are opposed to the biomedical paradigm of psychiatry. If you are one of them, I suggest that you visit this website: https://www.scientificfreedom.dk

If you have read this far, you may be left with a lot of questions.

"What am I supposed to do, then? If I quit the drugs, won't I return to the same state I was in?"

Just like a snowflake, you are unique. There is nobody else who is "you." I have some suggestions that may help, but it is up to you to pick what fits.

Don't allow others to judge you. Select your crowd. If you have poisonous people in your environment – take a break from them. When someone says, "you can't do this" they are saying "I can't do this."

Are you "depressed" or simply surrounded by asshats?

Don't buy into the trauma-trap. We all have had adverse experiences. And you have a choice:

> Will you let your worst moments define the trajectory of the rest of your life, or the best ones? Will you let your diagnosis define you, or will you define your life?

Silvia Hartman is a spiritual teacher, and the founder and president of the Guild of Energists. She talks about our "Star Moments" – the times in your life that left you ecstatic. When you were flowing with the moment. These are more important than the darkness you have gone through. This is the love that fuels your life.

Am I saying it is easy? That there are no thorns in the rose garden?

Far from it.

I have attempted to finish my own life nine times. First time in 1983, last attempt in 2019. When I work with people with suicidal ideation, I don't speak only from a theoretical point of view. I know that it is so easy to create a pattern where ending your life becomes a viable option. Where you convince yourself that the world would be a better place without you. Your family will forget you, the world will move on, and you will find peace. That was what I thought.

This is not true. A suicide creates ripples of pain.

And we do know a lot about the causes. One major cause, something which has been prevalent in my own life, is money. My last attempt came when I lived in my car, had no money whatsoever, and social services and mental health said that they couldn't help me. A Swedish study from 2023 showed that 20% of Swedes who had problems with debt had tried suicide. Being poor is a taboo, and what we don't talk about doesn't change. Despite us knowing this, despite the worsening statistics, it seems that the governments of the world are afraid to act. In Norway, 70 more people chose to die in 2023 than in 2022.

I blame no-one for my problems. Though I must say that the drugs haven't helped. But I did what I did, and I take full responsibility for my own life choices, including the pain I have caused my family.

If you are feeling suicidal, please … don't think that you are alone. Reach out for help. An exercise I have used is ***"Wait One Minute."*** I first used it with a young man from a middle eastern country some years ago.

He asked me to come to his bedroom, and said "I will kill myself. I have prepared everything, and you can't stop me." I said "OK." He continued "you know my story, so you understand why." "I understand why" I responded. I asked him to lay down on his bed and take a deep breath. I then asked him to remember the traumatic memory. I said, "So you want to kill yourself. Can you wait one minute?" He smiled, a tear dripping onto his pillow, and nodded. I kept quiet for one minute. Then I said, "Can you repeat it?" He said yes. We waited for one more minute. "Can you wait ten minutes?" He laughed. After the ten minutes had gone by, I continued "So, you have shown that you can wait. Can you wait until tomorrow?" He gave me a hug, said he was tired, and asked me to sit in his room until he fell asleep. The next day we got him an appointment to see a psychiatrist, whom he met once.

He is still alive.

Our world is a living organism, and we are its caretakers. It's time to challenge the systems that profit from our illnesses and embrace holistic healing. Together, we can create a future where mental health is nurtured, not numbed.

This is my three-step method to happiness:

1. Find a love object. It can be a dog, a child, an artist, a humanitarian organisation, work or your idea of God.

2. Create a daily ritual where you show your love for this object.

3. Increase your love 1% each day and pay it forward.

I will leave you with a mantra, taken from Ho'oponopono: "I'm sorry. Please forgive me. Thank you. I love you.."

<3 Håkon/Hawk.

A poem:

I wrote this poem when I was in a psych ward 30 years ago. We had started with group therapy, and there were a lot of people who were hurting. So, I started writing poems and shared them in the group. Here's one:

The Black Light of Depression

If I could take your pain,

your depressions, neuroses, psychoses, and your anxiety

Wrap them neatly in rose petals and swallow them

So that you could have a holiday

A little break

Then I would have done so.

If I could have taken

your sorrow for things done and undone

your anxiety about living and dying

your anger over missed chances

for a little while

Then I would have done it.

But I cannot do that

I can offer you

a hand now and then, a small word occasionally

But you must live with your pain

It is a part of you

Without it, you are not you.

Does not the flowers of love shine brighter against a backdrop of sorrow?

Do not bright summer evenings glow more intensely after dark winter days?

Does not happiness become like a nova in the black light of depression?

Haakon's journey to therapy was woven into his very essence, born to a psychologist and a lecturer who painted his childhood with the hues of Freud, Jung, and Reich. Like a young sapling reaching for the sun, he delved into the Bible at four, seeking solace after his

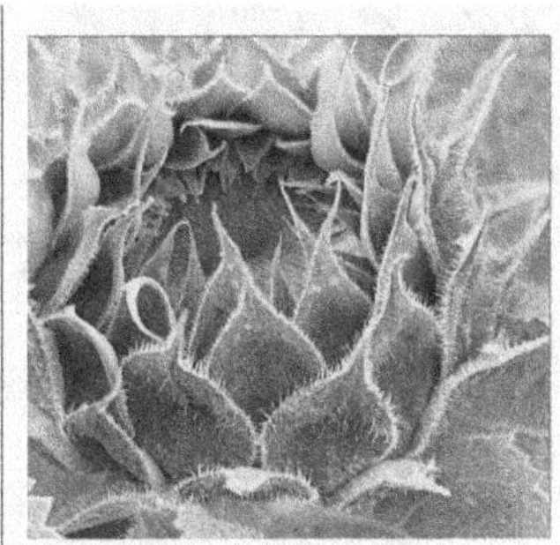

Feed me with sun, and I will become one!

father's departure a year before, and by 14, his mind had danced through half the local library. An ordained minister and Doctor of Divinity from the ULC, his academic roots took hold with a bachelor's in child welfare in 2008. He blossomed into a certified Tsa Lung healer in 2012, embraced the solitude of a celibate monk in 2019, and found harmony as a licensed holistic healer in 2020. With 22 years of therapeutically nurturing souls, he crafts healing melodies as "Mancient." Co-author #1 book, "Bullied: how I got by," a father to three and guardian of a loyal dog, Haakon invites you to explore his therapeutic garden at www.surroundtherapy.com or connect on LinkedIn at www.linkedin.com/in/mancient.

Doing Whatever It Takes

TONYA DAVIS ... A MOTHER'S JOURNEY

"Mom, I found my tribe." I stared at the joy on my son's face and my heart melted. His words echoed the sentiment I had been feeling all weekend but hadn't had a chance to voice. I felt the tears start to well up and I shoved them away. What a weekend it had been. Last year we had attended Nerdcore Party Con (NPC) but didn't really know what we were doing or what we were getting into. All I knew is we were driving six hours to Raleigh, North Carolina, for my kiddo, Brady, to watch one of his favorite Youtube creators, the one who started it all for us: Chewie Catt.

That trip began a year-long immersion into the world of Nerdcore. Every time we get in the car I hear the familiar question of, "Want me to get the music started, Mom?" I reply in the affirmative and off we go. Sometimes we just go to Dairy Queen or get snacks and take rides so that we can listen to the music. Or we're driving to a tennis clinic. It's our thing.

How could I tell he had found his tribe this year? Each day I watched him meet new people and talk excitedly about all the things they had in common. What movies they liked….their favorite creators there that weekend… whose autograph they wanted the most. Standing in line for an hour or more waiting to get into the venue sparked excited conversations with the kids while the adults tried to survive the heat.

I encountered several NPC moms that weekend and we all talked about how we had driven hours to give our kids this experience. We chuckled at our kiddos. They seemed oblivious to the heat. We focused on how worthwhile it was to support our kids in something they loved and felt connected to.

For those of you who aren't aware, a whole world exists where Youtubers create music related to games, fandoms, movies, etc. Some of these Youtubers have millions of subscribers. They come together once a year to perform their music and connect with their community. It is truly amazing to behold.

Everyone is accepted. Everyone is loved and for my son to feel so at-home brought tears to my eyes on more than one occasion. Of course, I never let him see. There's no crying at NPC, right? They all revel in coming together and being a part of a community that welcomes them with open arms.

I'll give a little bit of background on our NPC journey before I tell you my Rattled Awake moment in all of this. Last year when we attended, we really only knew

Chewie Catt and a few other creators who were vaguely on our peripheral radar. The day of the concert we had just walked in and were standing in the merch line. My son excitedly tapped me on the shoulder and was like "There he is Mom!" and there was Chewie Catt wandering around on the main floor. I took a picture from far away. He noticed and began walking toward us. He came over to say hi!

My son freaked out and was star struck. He didn't know what to say. Ok, I have to admit, I fangirled a little for my son and after he said hi to us, I found the words, "We are so excited to be here! We drove six hours just to watch you perform!" He shyly smiled and said, "Really? I just hope I don't forget the words." Such a nice guy. I responded with, "Oh I know you will do fantastic" or something similar to that.

Then the kiddo unfroze and began talking with him. I asked if we could get a picture and he was very gracious and acquiesced. That, my friends, was our introduction to NPC. And even though we only stayed for the first half of the concert because I cannot stand for 5 ½ hours, this moment alone made everything worth the six hour drive.

Fast forward a year and we were embarking on our second NPC. Having grown wiser, getting VIP seats so that momma can sit and enjoy the concert, we also got to attend the VIP party on Friday night. Right when we walked in there were creators interacting with fans. While standing in line to meet the first creator, my son and another young man began talking.

Again, seeing my son getting to talk with others who enjoy what he loves warmed my heart. We met so many creators that night alone and got pictures and he had great interactions with them. Just let me say that these youtubers love and appreciate their fans. They are gracious with their time and enjoy interacting with them. And they all remembered him two days later at the official meet and greet! That's why such a sense of community exists. Then we were treated to a special concert. That was where I met my first NPC mom.

We were standing on the steps watching the concert and she turned to strike up a conversation. Her son was a little older than mine, but we had in common the love for our kiddos and being there to support them. I also discovered we both have autoimmune disorders that don't make doing things like this easy. Throughout the weekend we would spot each other, shout out greetings, and wave.

My son had gone from being star struck and tongue-tied to approaching creators and talking with them a mile-a-minute. Talk about practicing social skills and getting out of your comfort zone. What a difference a year makes! One of the best parts of this story is yet to come. Don't worry dear readers, we will get there.

On the second day we got there early before the doors opened because I remembered how long it took us to get through the merch line. Lo and behold there was the young guy my kiddo had met. They picked up right where they left off and had a fabulous time talking back and forth. It ended up that they were going to the merch line and momma was gonna go stake out seats. I could see them from the upper balcony which meant I didn't have to stand in line. With fibromyalgia it's very difficult for me to stand or walk for long periods of time. So he got to gain some independence and I could be comfortable. Win-Win.

Truthfully, it has been a year of huge growth for both of us. I have worked hard at giving him more freedom. Being a part of the tennis team gave him tremendous confidence. He was able to spread his wings and do a lot more on his own. I will say though, it's been hard for this momma. On the one hand, I want him to be more independent so that he can go out and function in the world. On the other hand, it means he doesn't need me as much. Now he is more open to doing things out of his comfort zone. And when he doesn't need me I laughingly wonder to myself, have I done my job too well? In truth, this is what's supposed to happen. It's the natural order of things and I must accept it and nurture it. But if you are a parent and are struggling with the kiddos getting older, leaving the nest soon, I am right there with you. We can support each other. Yet, this is another reason why it's so important for him to find his path and his community.

When I say that Nerdcore is a community, it truly is. My son's new friend asked if I would watch his things since I would be sitting the whole time. I obliged, said I would do the mom thing and watch his stuff. Lol. I looked around and saw families with younger kids and people just enjoying being together in this electric atmosphere. You could feel the joy in the air.

During the concert I connected with two more moms, one on each side of me. We talked about our love for our children and how important they are to us. I was happy as a clam. Also, the amazing music and performances kept the energy up.The crowd never waned. They held the same energy from the first song all the way through the encore. Day two, and my son was over the moon. One more day to go.

We arrived early once again to get in line for the meet and greet day, and who did we run into? The same young man Brady had been hanging out with each day. A group of them clustered together and talked exuberantly about their common interests.

I began a conversation with what I fondly think of as an NPC mom. We marveled at how they connected and how much of a family event it truly is. She even talked about how nice it would be to have an area for the parents to hang out in together. What a great idea! NPC.....what do you think?

Full disclosure here. If you are thinking about taking your kiddo to NPC, please be aware that some of the songs do have some stronger language and, as it is a concert, there are adult beverages. But, I will tell you in the two years we have been there, I've never seen anyone get out of hand. Plus, I have always felt safe there.

On to the meet and greet, which was very organized this year. Thank you NPC! As we walked in we discovered a list of creators, times and what station they would greet fans. We had fun strategizing, making a game plan to make sure he could meet all the creators he really wanted to see. There just wasn't time to meet all 21 of them.

As we moved through each creator's line I donned the role of NPC mom once again. Kiddo even got me a t-shirt with the title displayed. He formed a friendship with some guys standing behind us in line. I tried to give him his space but interjected a comment every once in a while. My presence was not only tolerated but well received. Still, I wanted him to have his time with his new buds. It was then that we came to the moment when he told me, "Mom, I found my tribe."

Now, if you are a parent reading this, I'm sure you worry about your kiddos. I worry about mine being healthy and happy. Part of that worry is wondering where he will end up for a career. You see, for nine years I helped build a non-profit that bridged the gap between education and employment for students. I provided experiences to help the students connect to employers and learn about careers so they could decide if they truly wanted to pursue that career. I loved what I did but had to step away due to my autoimmune disorder. For more on that story please refer to "Rattled Awake: Volume Four," where I talk about my decision to leave.

I want Brady to be happy in what he's doing. I know money isn't everything, but I do want him to be comfortable enough to make a living doing what he loves. When he told me he found his tribe, I knew he was meant to be a part of this world. I have held off the coolest meet and greet experience until now. We'll come back to his happiness and career momentarily.

You see, for the last three years I have held Tik Tok lives on Monday's at 9pm EST. We talk about our growth and work on affirmations. I have cultivated a supportive community there and the kiddo comes in at 9:30 to give us an intermission. What started out as him coming in a dino costume to jump around and make us laugh has evolved into emoting performances with an LED mask to NPC music.

Before NPC began, we went onto the beach (garnering some interesting looks mind you) and he performed a song of Chewie Catt's with his mask.The child who was so tongue tied and star struck he could barely speak to Chewie Catt the year before SHOWED HIM this video at the meet and greet. I cannot tell you how proud I was of him!

My heart swelled as ChewieCatt said to him, "Is this you????" and when Brady affirmed it was him, Chewie Catt replied, "Bro, that's sick!" Another creator, Zach B, stood behind them so I panned out to get his reaction and you can see the other creator saying, "That's so cool." Kiddo asked permission to upload the performance and Chewie Catt told him he didn't mind at all. If you want to see the interaction it's pinned on my Tik Tok page. I think that was the single greatest moment of his life to date.

Now that I have given you the backstory to his journey, I'm going to tell you how I landed at my Rattled Awake moment. Since I retired, (I'm only 50) due to this autoimmune issue I have struggled on my own path. I've found ways to continue to help people which I believe is my mission on this earth. But I will tell you, dear readers, the struggle has been real. I had yet to find my flow until this past month.

I just couldn't seem to get traction to start a business. I felt like blocks kept coming up and a huge one emerged out of nowhere. To make a long story short we ended up having to get a new car for my step-daughter unexpectedly. Trust me, she needed the car but as things happen with parents, the extra income I had planned on using for my business now needs to be allocated there. She's in nursing school, has found her tribe and I couldn't be happier for her. She has found her path and is killing it!

How and when she needed the car was a perfect storm that couldn't be helped as so often happens in life. I was totally discouraged on that day as to what to do now. Then my Rattled Awake moment hit me like a lightning bolt. I only have three years left with my son before he graduates and goes out into the world. My time is not to be spent on a business for myself, but to help him as much as I can while he is here to "launch" him as I call it....getting him started on his path. All I did for my previous job was networking for students. I can do this for my son! A weight lifted from my shoulders and I knew in my heart this is what I am meant to do.

How to get started? First, we are working to get him back to NPC next year. Instead of it taking place in North Carolina, it's going to be in Dallas next year which presents a lot of barriers but we are going to make it happen.

Until then, he and I have talked about starting a podcast. When your teenage son wants to do a podcast with you, as a parent, you *jump* at the chance. We can talk about our NPC journey, how things are going in life, and offer support to teenagers and parents along the way. Since I made that shift things have begun to flow confirming my decision. Think about it, Lonnee called me spur of the moment and asked me to be involved in this Rattled Awake edition. That conversation evolved into my telling this story, and ended-up with my son being a contributing author! Talk about being in the flow, right?

How does this relate to mental health, you might ask? My hope is that our journey will inspire parents and their kids to work together to find careers that they love. Knowing our children are on the trajectory they are meant to be on decreases our stress and anxiety. We can help parents give their children the personal experiences needed to help them find their way on their career journey.

My own mental health has had such a shift just in the last month knowing that my kiddo needs to be in the world of NPC somehow. Some way. Now we have a goal to work towards. I feel lighter knowing that going in this direction will get him where he needs to go. For the kids, they can be happy in a career they love. I always told the students find what you are passionate about then we will figure out a career for it. When we are following our passions our mental health is better, we function better, and we are happier.

If you as a parent need help supporting your children just let us know. I want you as a parent to have decreased stress about the happiness of your children. For the kiddos, I want them to have less stress as they are exploring their careers and finding their own career journey that will lead to happiness. Stay tuned for our podcast __(TBA)___ coming out soon. Follow us on our journey and hopefully it will inspire you and your kiddo too!

If you have questions about how as a parent you can support your child please reach out to me on Linked In or Tik Tok. I would love to talk with you further!

Tonya Davis is on a mission to support her son in discovering his passion and finding his hopes and dreams. She has spent the last 25 years using her passion for supporting others as a way to guide them on their road to prosperity. Whether it be health or wealth, she offers many tools and experiences to achieve a happy balance. After spending nine years assisting in building a non-profit whose intention was to bridge the gap between education and employment for students, she realized what better way to help her own child than with the knowledge and skills she learned during that time. Along the way she hopes to inspire other parents in supporting their children on their own career journeys to help them find a career they are passionate about. Be on the lookout for an upcoming podcast relaying our journey!

Linked In: https://www.linkedin.com/in/tonya--davis/

TikTok: https://www.tiktok.com/@smurfette747?_t=8p75se3RG2N&_r=1

Pursue Your Biggest Dreams

BRADY ANDERSON ... MY NERDCORE JOURNEY

I remember several years ago me and my friends playing a game during the pandemic because we had literally nothing to do at the time. At one point one of my friends sent me a video. It was a song about the game we were playing. This would be my introduction to Nerdcore. The song was, "Collided," by Chewiecatt. I hadn't known it just yet but years later I would recognize this as the song that would also be the start of my Nerdcore journey.

Years later I would be on Chewiecatt's youtube page and see an announcement about his participation in something called Nerdcore Party Con (NPC.) Imagine my excitement! I had no idea that Nerdcore artists performed live. I came to learn NPC is a three day convention ending in a meet and greet, which is a big reason why a lot of people attend. I, however, was ignorant to all of this at the time. How could I have known, with my limited knowledge of the nerdcore community, that this could be a thing. My only knowledge of the community was Chewiecatt and a minor exposure to the group of people, Nerdout. I thought it would just be a concert. This turned out to be the happiest mistake I'd ever made. I really had no idea how much NPC, and the people involved, would come to mean to me.

NPC is more than just a fun convention. It's where I can meet and find people who are interested in the same things as me, but so much more. For our first day, we went to the concert and at first I had no idea what was going on. Then Chewiecatt came on. I was SO happy and excited.

The next day me and my mom waited in line for hours and keep in mind, at this point I barely knew any artists there. I knew who Chewiecatt is and I listened to one or two songs by a group of three guys called Nerdout. I'd only heard of somebody called Zach B because he was on a collaboration with Chewiecatt, and I'd heard of somebody called CG5. Needless to say, I was unaware of just how big this community was.

Before the concert, me and mom were waiting in line to get Chewiecatt merch. As we're standing there I saw a beanie. I was shocked and frozen. Chewiecatt often wears a beanie. Could it be him? When he turned around I recognized him and immediately started flipping out inside. All I could do was tap on my mom's shoulder rapidly and repeat the phrase, "Mom, that's him," over and over again. I had no idea what to do other than that. My memory of that moment is relatively blurry in terms of how we started talking to him. All I remember is being so starstruck I couldn't speak.

Remembering the interaction now, I think I said hi while my mom completely fangirled over him. 'This was so cool!' kept running through my head. I thought it would be the best moment of the night except for when he would perform. Unfortunately, they were out of Chewiecatt merch so I got a Nerdout shirt (which I still have to this day.)

When the concert started, me and mom were introduced to how insane Nerdcore music can get. The first person to start the concert off was an artist called Peso Pete. My mom constantly says she recognizes if a song was made by him, not by his voice, but how many times the F bomb is dropped in the song. I find her reaction to be utterly hilarious, but from now on, I skip those songs when mom is around. Fast forward a few acts and Chewiecatt hit the stage. The first song he did was, at the time, my favorite song of his. I was singing the song along with him, Nerdout, and Zach B as that was the only song I knew Zach B from at the time.

After Chewiecatt's segment ended we were introduced to somebody named JT Music. JT Music would become the catalyst for my expansion of knowledge in terms of the nerdcore community. Through JT Music I would now be listening to someone other than Chewiecatt, religiously. There weren't a lot of notable things that happened at that meet and greet beyond meeting another artist, GameboyJones, whom I would listen to later on down the line.

Little did I know that this first NPC event would change the course of my music tastes forever. It also opened my eyes to how big the community really was.

Summer ended and school began. The only good thing about that was I could listen to music when nothing was going on throughout the day. Now that my mind was open to the nerdcore community, I logged on Spotify and my nerdcore playlist was born. Sticking with just a few artists, I added the likes of Rustage, Shao dow, and Cam Steady.

Slowly, over time, these creators, among others, would be the ones I listened to a lot. The only caveat was since I didn't have a Spotify premium account, I couldn't choose, only hope to hear, some of my favorite songs. I always joked with my friend that my goal was to make this playlist long enough that it would last the whole school day, seven hours. As of typing this story, my playlist is sitting at 16 hours and 33 minutes... and will likely grow longer between now and when you're reading this.

Eventually, I got Spotify premium. It fueled my drive to find people I really liked in the community since I could choose the song. Over time this playlist would continue to grow and I'd discover some other people who I'd listen to occasionally and others who I'd get really into like Daddyphatsnaps, (yes, that's his name), Rustage, JT Music, Shao Dow, Cam Steady, and Game Boy Jones. Soon, it was time to attend my second NPC, held in Myrtle Beach, SC.

For my birthday, I asked for an LED mask. My Tik Tok account was doing pretty well and I wanted to up my game. Then a thought occurred to me, "Hey, I could use the mask for mom's intermission on Tik Tok and make it more fun." I knew mom's Tik Tok people would be excited to see the mask because her community is very accepting. I was right. It was a hit! Eventually I transitioned to using only Nerdcore songs for the intermissions and uploading videos to youtube. Before attending the second NPC, I filmed and uploaded two videos at the beach. I was excited for the meet and greet this year because one of them was a Chewiecatt song that I so desperately wanted to show him, but we'll get to that a little later.

We'd been at Myrtle Beach prior to the concert and when I tell you I was hyped, I mean I was hyped. I listened to my Nerdcore playlist the whole way there. This time we had VIP tickets; you best believe I was excited.

Typically, at the VIP party, there are a few people who perform before the main concert the next day. While we're in line we meet this guy and we're talking and when it's his turn to see Stupdendium I think to myself, "Well that was fun. Shame I probably won't see him again." Little did I know, I would definitely be seeing him again.

As the VIP party continued I met Chewiecatt again and am proud to say I'd actually managed to get more words out than just, "hi." Me, him, and mom talked for a while, which was fun. Plus, I was getting this feeling, like I wasn't quite alone as I once thought I was. As the night went on I met more artists. Mom and I went up to the second level of the place and I spotted somebody. I was sitting there thinking, "Is that Shao dow? No. Surely it's not." I'm talking to my mom almost as if thinking out loud. She eventually just tells me to go over and ask so I did. It turned out it was him, and we ended up talking for a little bit.

We met a few other people, then took positions on a staircase that allowed us to get a good, clean view of the mini-concert. I had such a blast!

Remember how I mentioned the guy before that I thought I wouldn't see again? The next day, he was at the end of the line to get into the concert, too, so we got to talk again! Since we had VIP seats we decided mom would watch the guy's bag. To lessen confusion we'll call him Kestis, after a jedi, because I'm a nerd.

So me and Kestis decided to go to the merch line. While we're in line they're doing sound checks to make sure the technology is working. Cam Steady sound checks a song called, "Pokemon Villain Cipher" which was the second Pokemon cypher I found and is one my favorites.

Eventually somebody comes through and literally parts Kestis and I, says, "I'm so sorry" quite desperately. Me and Kestis are just left laughing at the fact that this happened and since then, I've repeatedly pretended to respond to the guy, saying, "Dude, I'm sorry. I have no idea what I did but I feel like I'm the one who did it" while laughing.

Finally we get our merch and see Chewiecatt again. Lemme tell ya, if you ever go there, you will find him everywhere and that is a good thing to me because I really like talking to him. Kestis also talked to him because

Rustage, one of the artists, has a card game that Kestis had a deck for. His goal was to get every artist there to sign a card. If I remember correctly he said that he'd achieved his mission, which I thought was really cool.

After some time he told me his plan. He wanted to reach the front row so that he could be there when Rustage, his favorite, started performing. The problem was we weren't sure that we could make it up there as he was the third artist up. We were still very close to the front though. Finally, the concert finally started. The first act is a duo of artists that go by Rockit Music. One of the songs they performed was based on a video game that has the avatar as a hazmat! I was shocked and thought it was a bold choice considering how hot the room was.

Either the next song or the song after, one of their songs involved throwing toilet paper into the crowd. I ended up getting hit in the back of the head which to this day I think is hilarious. Later on they would also throw a plunger, a part of the same song. The person who caught the plunger would hold into the air like a sword. It was as if he was rallying the crowd to war. to this day, if I think about it, it will make me laugh just because of how random it was.

Soon after Rockit Music left, JT Music came on stage! I remember in the group that Kestis and I were in, I was the only person who'd cheered as enthusiastically as I did. I felt a little embarrassed which quickly changed after the song started. The performers just kept coming! Rustage performed one of my favorite songs and I was very excited about that even though we hadn't reached the front row.

After Rustage's performance Kestis and I would once again separate. He'd gone to get food and wanted to make sure he could get to the front row. But Chewiecatt was the next act so I had a different plan. I saw the set list and knew that the second half was going to be crazy on the floor so my plan was to stay down there until Chewiecatt performed. Then I would join mom in the VIP seats before returning to the floor, then stay down there for the whole second half.

And then Chewiecatt came on. It was so exciting seeing the man who got me into Nerdcore performing live on stage! He again played my favorite song and, as planned, returned to sit with mom. A little while after I went back down to the floor; it was time for the second half to start. The energy on the floor was very hyped and felt fiery!

As Shao Dow came on the stage I saw he was wearing a cool flag with his logo on it. He crowd surfed on his stomach rather than his back. It was hilarious because the adults around me all had similar reactions of, "Oh he's doing that wrong," with very uncomfortable expressions like they're imagining what's happening. Mom and I were a bit caught off guard when Shawbadi played "Blood Brothers" because it was so aggressive. It was funny talking about it afterwards with mom because of mom's reaction. She was completely and utterly shocked because when we met him he was so chill.

Cam Steady came out in an armor cosplay suit which looked amazing! At the end of his segment of the concert he ended up crowd surfing and I was very close to where he was in the crowd! I actually ended up almost being under him while he crowd surfed, 'correctly,' I might add. Gameboy Jones literally apologized before and after one of his songs. I'm not going to be getting into detail about the song, but during one part I thought, "Oh god I have to go back up to mom after this."

When the last act hit the stage I was hyped. I knew what came next. The Living Tombstone would perform what the community considers the theme song of FNAF (Five Nights at Freddy's.) It was GLORIOUS! Better than I could've possibly imagined and I sang every word. I raced back up to mom's seat for the encore. Every single artist who had performed that day and the night before all sang the Pokemon theme song. Dear god, it was amazing! I sang every lyric and my mom was confused for the first few seconds. At least until it got to the words and mom was finally able to figure out which song it was. She knew I would be so happy to get to hear that song.

Finally, we reached the hotel and I knew my voice would be shot for the next few days. I wondered if I would see Kestis tomorrow. I sure hoped so. I wanted to get his Instagram or something to stay in touch because there's not a lot of people in my area that are into Nerdcore. I wanted to have some way to talk to somebody who was.

Who did I see when we got to the meet and greet line on the final day? You guessed it, Kestis. Out of the blue Cam Steady comes up and offers everybody near him bracelets. Mom managed to snag me and Kestis a bracelet each. I'm actually wearing it as I type this out.

So, as the meet and greet was going on, I went up to Chewicatt's station. As I mentioned earlier, I wanted to show him the video I made using his song and my LED mask. I felt a little nervous but excited at the same time. He thought the video was really cool. Man, that gave me a massive confidence boost. This community is an amazing community and I am so glad to be in it even if I don't make my own music yet; even if I just listen to these amazing artists. But maybe one day....

You know what one of the cool things
is about NPC? The people.

Just while standing in line to meet Daddyphatsnaps, I met some guys and we talked about anime and Star Wars....once again, community. I met Daddyphatsnaps at the meet and greet. This man gives some of the best hugs in the world which was confirmed by the guy behind me saying, "Man I hope he hugs me again." After a while I saw an artist named Johnald just walking around. I thought it was awesome that I got his signature. I met Nerdout, a really good group of people. While in line for a different artist they did a Make-a-Wish event. One of the artists did a freestyle which I recorded and will occasionally listen to because it was good; it makes me feel good inside.

This community is honestly one of the best out there.

I know because I am part of a lot of fandoms that have big communities. Unfortunately, they are very often toxic. The nerdcore community is so supportive of everything and everybody. Everybody from the artists to the fans are all so kind and caring and everybody in that community is an amazing person from what I've seen. All of the people I've met are so amazing and the community is truly amazing. The impact this experience has had on me is hard to describe and I look forward to seeing how this helps me continue as a creator.

When I'm there I don't feel alone. I truly found my tribe, my community, my people.

Brady Anderson is on a mission to share his experiences at Nerdcore Party Con (NPC) as a way to show others how they too can find their tribe. He wants them to know they are not alone and they can always find support. Given the right tools they too can connect to things they love and are passionate about. Sharing his story can bring hope and help others who need it. Brady has attended NPC for the last two years and hopes to be a performer himself one day.

TikTok:

https://www.tiktok.com/@mountain_state_rapper?_t=8p75cTtUD0N&_r=1

Youtube:

https://youtube.com/@suprgamr6652?si=dOQVaFGgLZkOHU3n

Peace Please Let Me Be

LONNEE REY ... BULLIES AND SUICIDE

My mother knew she was intuitive so she moved to get training in Cassadega, (House of God), AKA: "PsychicVille." Walking down the street of her mobile home park one day, my brother nudged me hard, saying, "Sis! Sis! Think 'carport carport carport carport' right now!" It seemed an odd way to treat his visiting big sis, but okaaaay…

"Sis," he said, "These people read your thoughts. Repeating that word clears your mind and throws them off – unless you want them to know your every thought. You gotta block it, trust me, Sis, I've lived here five years."

◆ ◆ ◆

Like it or not, people can read thoughts. They can even go so far as to insert thoughts and affect behavior.

It's easy: via repetition, a core tenant of brainwashing. "Safe and effective," for example, now the 'Swiss cheese' of our times, was repeated ad nauseum. It makes drug pushers (Big Harma) a ton of cash. Over time, slogans can become white noise. They seep into the subconscious and, like a squatter, take up residence in your mind as an unquestioned belief system. Since we take actions based on our beliefs, I believe we need to be more vigilant about keeping an open mind to new ideas while simultaneously questioning mainstream narratives.

◆ ◆ ◆

Anyhoooo...

Six years later, our mother's training turned into a career as a medium. I jokingly called her The Reluctant Medium. (Catchy title; not-so-hot for business.) "No one goes to Cassadega hoping their talent is being able to access dead people's spirits," she said. Alas, that was her gift. She could "give it" to anyone except close family. Proximity, they say, muddies the clarity of reading for kinfolk.

My mother took calls at home, exclusively. On the odd day she left her dark cave, Ripley's Believe It Not would be notified. "Ellie braves heatwave to visit metaphysical bookstore," the Daytona Beach News would report. Suffice it to say, running into Ellie was about as likely as winning the lottery.

So when a grieving mother bumped into my hermit mother at the corner of "Past Lives" and "Creating Futures" in the bookstore, both were shocked. "I heard about you," the stranger said. "I would like to see you please."

Thrusting her business card into the woman's hand, my mother made a hasty exit. "Phone appointments only. Got to run."

In all her years doing phone readings, my mother never *ever* let someone come to her house. It must have been the beseeching, bereaved mother's call that got to her. "Please, my son just committed suicide and I need to see you. I just can't do this over the phone. PLEASE."

Mom bent the rules and allowed the woman to visit. Sitting across the table from each other, my mother began to deliver messages so detailed that the woman knew it was her son. Suddenly, an unseen force picked my mother up by the throat, forced her to stand up, and held her high up on the wall. Then, he dropped her. THUD! Mom's sixty-year-old ankle twisted into a really bad sprain.

"Suicided spirits are caught in between realms, confused by the death," she later told me. "He was very angry on top of being confused. Her son will be stuck in-between for a while. It's a really uncomfortable place for a disembodied spirit to be." It was really uncomfortable for her, too. Who knew such a thing could happen? For decades, she brought messages from beyond, and peace to her clients.

Ellie promptly removed her business cards from the community boards and told the bookstore not to refer her to anyone else ever again. She said, "The best thing we can do for a suicide is to tell them what happened, and that it is OK to go now. Our grief keeps them here, prolonging their soul's journey and release from the earthly plane of existence."

Dear reader, our job is to let them go just the same as any other passing. Judging them from the grave is not helpful, to say the least. All too often we hear "suicide is selfish." If you have never been that low, so lost for hope of anything getting better, you may be quick to repeat that trite expression. Allow me to explain: Someone in that 'position' cannot see past the toes of their shoes. The future looks darker than you can ever imagine. You have no idea what precipitated their feelings of hopelessness… futility…self-loathing. You have no idea how many years they have struggled, or why.

My parents were bullies. It really seemed like the best thing I could do was die. I was sure they would be happier without me around. I was just eight years old when I took way too many baby aspirin one night. I thought I was doing the world a favor. The same thoughts ran through my head as an adult, precipitating self-harm or suicidal ideations..

Know/No they are not trying to be selfish – they are in so much pain they don't know what else to do. Many who have survived suicide attempts have admitted they did not want to die – they just wanted the pain to stop.

Sticks and stones may break my bones
but bullying can be deadly.

Bullying, especially by more than one person, is a psychic attack. It literally diminishes a person's defenses to the point where their only escape from the relentless attacks and pain appears to be death.

A shocking 75% of people who witness bullying will join in with the bully. What the hell?! If you want to help prevent suicides from happening, stop a bully in their tracks. Do not condone their behavior. Walk away. Better yet, walk toward the fallen and help them get back up off the ground.

In 2019, I was bullied by people I thought to be my friends and team mates. We'd joined forces to co-create a chapter book. Unfortunately, the project heads delivered an embarrassment of a book. The only person to see any of the 100 advance copies I'd purchased was the trash man. Why was I the only one bold enough to call out the lies and liars for their wrongdoing? The group shunned, ridiculed, ostracized and criticized ME, instead.

The shock, disappointment and relentless public attacks took me down hard one night. I was sobbing so hard I don't know how I 'heard' it: "Just quit. This is what your life is going to be like. Just quit." I'm not sure where that voice came from, but it felt true: my life had been a series of 'almost made it' moments. The epic fail of the book, combined with the betrayal and bullying, was too much. I gave in to the voice, agreed my life was never going to amount to anything, and I should just stop trying. To those of you who have been bullied, you know exactly how I felt that night: hopeless AF. "Why bother?" is unanswerable; an endless loop. It might as well be a hangman's noose.

That night, I gave up. *You win. I hope you're happy now.*

The 30+ sleeping pills began to take effect. Banging

against the walls, struggling to make it to my bed before I collapsed, a different voice spoke to me. "OH! You quit too soon! You quit too soon!!" WTF. I can't even kill myself right. I'd heard you get to choose your 'exit ramp' and this was mine. Leave me alone. I was pissed and shouted, "I quit too soon?!! According to whom? According to what?! Why can't I see the goddamn manual?!" Silence. "OHHHH!! You quit too soon! You quit too soon!"

"FINE!! On the outside chance I just fucked-up, and there is more for me to do – that maybe my life will get better – angels, wake me up in the morning." I figured there was no way that could happen and I would finally see the end of a life wrought with struggles. I threw in "Jesus take the wheel" and called it done.

A near-death experience when I was 12 years old proved that dying is not something to be afraid of. In fact, pulling out of your body is really peaceful.

That night wasn't a cry for help, it was resignation. I was tired of the battle. The bullies beat the life out of me. Game over. Good-bye cruel world…catch ya on the flipside. My old friends would know to be happy for me – I got out. No doubt the bullies would be satisfied in snuffing out a person they delighted in destroying.

My portable speaker played my funeral song on repeat. "Silence" by Tiesto and Sarah MacLachlan https:// youtu.be/qycAC_6Bbto?si=5LcFjrX7ztCg0tQ_

"Give me release

Witness me

I am outside

Give me peace

Heaven holds a sense of wonder
And I wanted to believe that I'd get caught up
When the rage in me subsides"

I clutched the speaker and quickly fell asleep…

Have you ever woken up talking? Had a dream so real that you thought it was really happening? That night, I had a dream that my good friend was standing at the foot of my bed. I woke up talking to her, sat up, looked for her, realized it was just a dream, and fell back down. Then it happened again: woke up, sat up, took a breath to speak to her, realized it was just a dream, and fell back down to die. It happened a third time, exactly the same way.

If I were going to live at all, it would be days before I woke up…or so I thought. At 8AM, I woke up, sat up, and put my feet on the floor. I wasn't groggy, sick, or hung over. It was as if nothing ever happened.

"OK, fine. I guess there is more for me to do." I thought back to the time before my near-death experience. I was 11 years old, taking a flight to see my bestie in NJ. I loved flying, so when I found myself suddenly terrified that the plane was going to crash, it was really out of character. Fear like that never gripped me so fiercely – I was sure that I was having an intuitive hunch and the plane was going to crash. Then, out of nowhere, I heard a voice say, "Don't worry. It's not your time yet." It was so loud I looked around to see who said it. There was no one sitting next to me, though. And how could anyone know what I was thinking? Glancing back over the airplane's wing, panic hit twice as hard. "Don't worry, it isn't your time yet," the voice said, much louder this time. So, I did what any kid would do: hit the overhead buzzer, asked the stewardess for a Coke, sat back and enjoyed the ride.

Was I going to be able to enjoy 'the ride' this time? Was life going to get any easier? If "you have more to do" equated to more struggles, where the past equaled the future – what was the point? Why did this happen at all?? Was it so I could bare my soul to you right now? Was it so that if you ever find yourself in the same boat you will ask the angels, or Jesus, to help you?

Dear reader, I have no idea why I was saved that night. Things have not been a bed of roses since that miracle happened. Convid hit, ruined my tiny import business, and then I got fired for taking on a group of cancel-culture bullies on Facebook. Who knew they were the adult children of my then-boss? Jeez Louise. He threatened to stab me in both eyes with forks if I ever spoke badly about his kids. Nice. Ironically, a few years later, he was the first to call them out for their willful ignorance. No, no apology ever came from him. It takes a big man to admit his mistake.

Did I survive so I could help people get their messages published? Was that always the plan? Is that why the voice said I quit too soon? I have no idea. Truth is this past year has been filled with all manner of abuse and pain (physical, mental, spiritual and financial), despair and disappointment. Good things have happened, too: I won the lottery on the date I thought it would happen. My client's book won "Best Indie Book of the Year, 2023." A dozen best-selling "Rattled Awake" style chapter books have been published, within days after a writer's workshop, in the past 12 months. The strangest things have manifested out of the blue proving, over-and-over, there is a power in each of us to create what we want. It takes vision, dedication and action. These are the only way to alter and manifest different outcomes for ourselves.

It is amazing what you can do when you don't know you can't.

People need encouragement like a plant needs water. Yet, when 75% of people are quick to join the bully, not help the bullied, it can feel like the whole world is against you. People who profess to be your friends turn out to be full of it. It sucks – *they* suck – but YOU don't.

Don't let the turkeys get you down, Honey. Look up David Goggins on YouTube. He is fierce and calls it like he sees it. The comments sections are filled with haters. Why? Because he rose up? Because he is still winning, beating the odds and successful? Is that a reason to hate on someone? Yes, when a person is a hammer, everything looks like a nail. But to those who know how hard it is to keep taking punches from the peanut-gallery, and prevail, he is their hero. Check him out.

Trying to stay up in an upside-down world ain't easy, I know. Don't give up; it's not your time, yet. So press the buzzer, grab a Coke, and enjoy the flight. This, too, shall pass.

And finally, **to the bullies** out there who think they are justified in their torment, read about Dolly in the best-seller, "Bullied: How I got by...stories from people who have lived to tell about, literally." Her father invited his daughter's bullies to her funeral. Does it really take seeing someone's death by suicide to change your ways??

I KNOW WE CAN HELP PREVENT SUICIDES FROM HAPPENING BY TAKING A STAND AGAINST BULLYING.

Will you be the one who says NO MORE next time?

Lonnee Rey works as a facilitator of dreams, making them come true for people who do not know how to write, but hope to become a published author someday. Her transformational writing workshops, story coaching skills and use of paintbrush words help others take a chapter out of their lives and discover their message for the masses.

To date, she has published 14 books, all best-sellers, with a dozen of them being accomplished in the past year alone. The nearly-70 writers have gone on to write their own books, do their own anthology series, 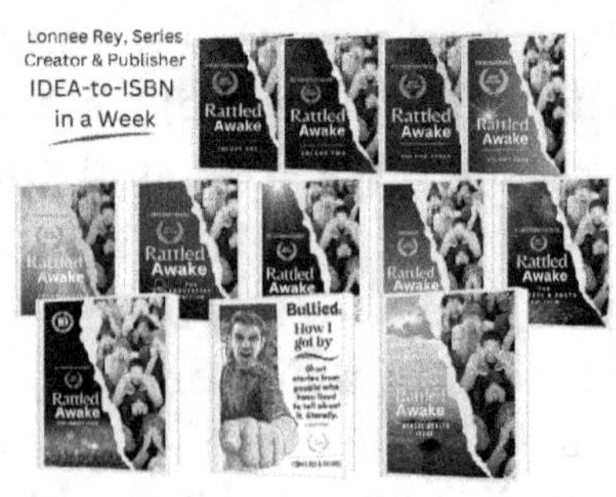

start YouTube channels, grow their podcasts and become

inspirational speakers.

A 2023 BIBA Award-winning editor, "Best Indie Book of the Year," her most difficult and impactful project so far is this book, published August, 2024. Please share this and help save someone's life. Available now on Goodreads and Amazon

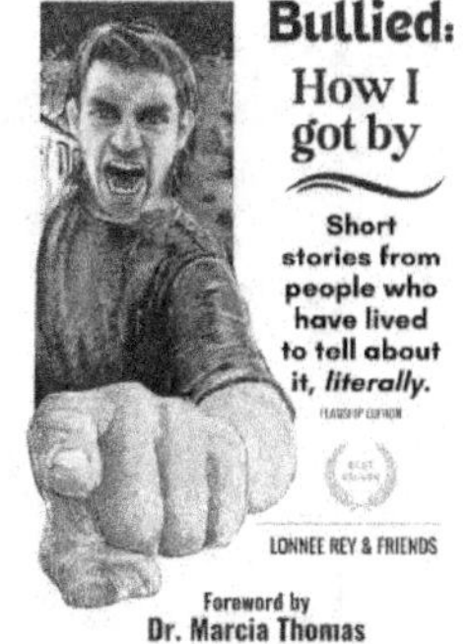

Do you have a book in you? Get in touch with her to discuss your ideas today.

https://www.officialrattledawake.com/

 **Wheee!** 

LONNEE REY ... "CHEAPER THAN THERAPY" PLAYLIST

Freebies to help you reset your mind and mood. Taken from my book, "How to Deal with a Dumbass: what to do and say when they come your way," now on Amazon. It waswritten to help recognize trouble before it becomes your problem, citing five red flags that will tip you off. When those people peeve you off, try doing something from this list to get back to center.

Since everybody recommends meditation, you won't find it mentioned. It works, but when you feel upset, sitting down to cite 'aum' might not be an option.

1. *Ask, "How can I have more fun today than I ever thought possible?"* Your brain works to answer the questions you ask of it, so use *this* one to reset the rest of your day. It's effortless and it works. The reason you want to get back to "fun" is so your creativity can flow, your vibe stays high, and your ability to handle a dumbass is enhanced. Ask this question any time, or any number of times in the day when you feel derailed.

2. *Tunes!* Play music that moves you. I go for "Na na na, hey, hey, hey," "No Time" by the Guess Who, and "Red Clay" by the hick-hop group, Jawga Boyz. You might love swing music. Whatever it is, make sure you choose upbeat, not sad, OK? Then put your fav on repeat. Who cares?? Use it to elevate you ASAP. Let it take you to a happy place. TO DO: start building that go-to music playlist this week.

3. *Rebuild your faith in YOU*. Confirm your ability to manifest! Look around you and notice all that you have manifested. You are powerful no matter how you feel right now. Delight in your own power to transform; know that you can handle this. Look for evidence in your life already - of how you've managed manifest outcomes in your favor before and you can do it again.

4. *Tapping.* See "Car Accidents" chapter for background on this helpful technique. Become your own healer by learning the 5 minute tapping routine. A near fix-all for most issues, (anxiety, pain, phobias, sadness) it will help whether or not you believe it will. This technique is easy to learn and you can do it anywhere, pretty much. Here is the 5 minute routine: https://youtu.be/Q8yVih75Wc4?si=tLhJ60xTh5geY9ql.

5. *Gift yourself with a present.* THE present. "NOW" is all we have. If you catch yourself reviewing or even futuring an interaction with a dumbass, get back to the 'here and now.' I find that consciously breathing in the word 'Light' and exhaling 'love' really helps. Pick words that work for you. Be really *really* present. Some folks write or say 10 gratitudes out loud. This puts you in the moment, too. Revisit #1 to reset your day's vibe.

6. *Sound off.* Let's face it, the sound of leaf blowers outside might be enough to put you over the edge. Or someone's voice - a song or a beat - these can get under your skin worse than a freakin' tick. It's time to change the channel. Sitting in the car, where sound is minimized, *with the stereo on*, works pretty well for a temporary escape. The bottom line: *adjust.* For sensitive types like us, sounds can truly make you squirm. If it's someone's incessant talking then you've got to figure out how to shut 'em up without a squabble. It might mean you relocate but it'd be worth your sanity. Ask yourself, "Do I want more of this or less of this?" "This" might be the feeling or the source of irritation. What matters most is *you* getting centered once again.

7. *Cafe Amor.* Show yourself some love with a steaming cuppa. Make it special. Will it be tea, or tequila, darlin'? Who cares? I knew a man who boasted about quitting drinking when his children were little. That was 40 years ago. "I really *love* Scotch." Then have some Scotch, brother. If you were on your deathbed tomorrow would you be glad you denied yourself all these years, long after the kids have grown and left home? Doubt it.

8. *Put on some lipstick.* Ladies, this works. If you work from home, like I do, it's too easy to look like a slouch. When I feel like crap, I reach for the paisley bell bottoms, fluff up my new shag haircut to look 70s cool, cover the dark circles and put on some eyeliner. It's a form of self-love when you make yourself look a bit fancy, I think. Just do it for you and watch your mood improve. Fill up your own cup and you have more to give. It isn't selfish, *it's essential.*

9. *Vent.* Have a venting buddy!! the understanding is that you just vent, they just listen. No advice is given. Let 'er rip, baby! Here's another idea: physically slamming a cheap metal burner plate cover on the counter is actually quite rewarding for most all the senses. I mean it. Don't knock it til ya try it. The sound of smashing plates on a brick wall would be ideal, of course. That was my fantasy: a place you could go to rage out. I called it the A.R.C. - the Anger Release Center. I hear there are places like this nowadays: "rage bars." For one dollar, you can get three loud burner plates - have your way with those instead of someone you'd love to trash. **Cheap thrills, baby.** Get 'em when you can. It's your job to let that stuff go and get back to feeling UP ASAP.

10. *Take a walk on the wild side*. Nature rocks. Put your spine up against a tree trunk and ask the tree to remove your pain, stress, etc. Run those toes through some grass or plop down on the moss and take a break. Send your stress into the earth and watch it go to work. This even helps with physical pains, by the way. Watch the movie, *"Earthing."*

11. *Phone a friend*. Pick up the phone just to say hello, how are you, my friend? Focusing on others and also, being of service to others if you are up to it, works quickly to reset your mindset. Also, know that you don't have to hide just because you are not feeling freaking awesome. A true friend understands ups and downs.

12. *Invite Divine Intervention*. THIS saved my life. See chapter, "Bullies and Suicide" in this book. Invite Divine Intervention into your world and expect to be amazed. Ask for a clear sign if you are not sure about a person, place or thing you might do. Be willing to follow the signs so you can minimize regrets later.

13. *LOL.* Jumping baby goats, screaming sheep and cat videos are *hysterical. Dry Bar Comedy Channel* on YouTube is good, clean humor so you don't have to worry if the kids can hear it. *Laugh Planet* has good clips to get you laughing, as well. Random Acts of Kindness videos will restore your faith in humanity. Rescued animals reuniting with their rescuer can't help but make you say 'aww!' Check out *The Dodo.* For Netflix lovers: keyword "witty" or "irreverent" and then pick "witty comedies" or "irreverent award winning movies" to get a 'leg up' on your cinematic time-out.

14. *Breathe.* When rough seas hit we hit the deck and become shallow breathers. This restricts your soul, they say. IDK who "they" is but I do know this much: deep inhales, imagining light or love coming in with deep exhales, imagining all the stress leaving you, really works. Combine it with putting your bare feet on the earth. It's a great combo. Wim Hof, AKA: "The Ice Man" has breathing techniques you can easily do, right now, for free, that are game-changers. In fact, he has helped thousands of people with verifiable psychosis to completely heal themselves and toss out those medications. Wow!

15. *Ribbon Cutting Ceremony.* Ties that bind for a long time need to be cut, releasing that person and clearing up your energy field once again. Here is what you do: imagine yourself and the external person/source that is a royal pain in butt. Go ahead and call it what it is, OK? Give yourself permission to cut those cords between you. SEE the cord connecting you to that person. Then imagine a gigantic pair of scissors in your hands. You know, the kind they use at grand opening ceremonies to cut that ribbon? Yes, like that: oversized to the max. SEE your hands on the handles and cut that cord between you and them. WATCH them float away, getting smaller and smaller. Wave bubye to that shrinking image. Continue doing ribbon cuttings for any source of irritation or angst, be it past or present. Honestly, this works so well *and* you don't even have to understand it. Just do it. See #1, next.

16. *Write your heart out.* Writing gets 'it' out of your head and onto paper where you can better deal with 'it.' Write letters you will never send. Let your emotions rage, roar and reveal how you truly feel. You gotta let it out to get it out. Have your say and be on your way. My book, "Life lessons learned from a lousy mother," was inspired by the time I tried to write a Mother's Day card of gratitude for all the wonderful things my mother taught me. I couldn't think of anything. It was blank. While that was a sad truth, it was acknowledging how I really felt…and *then* healing can fill the place of the release. Once you 'have' something you can let it go. **This book will help anyone with family issues that interfere with mental health/well-being.**

17. *Listen to a podcast.* Push away from your desk, (or that person) and tune into something else for a bit. If you'd like to hear a laugh that makes you laugh, check out these short episodes, contagious laughter and insights based on the book by the same title: https:// podcasters.spotify.com/pod/show/ howtodealwithadumbass

18. *Follow your "BIG Yes!"* It might defy logic or seem crazy to other people, but it works out in your favor. Your BIG Yes! might not be evident at this moment - the one where you've gotten blown off course or blown-away by somebody's 'stuff.' That's OK. When in doubt, wait it out. **Delete the need to understand**. Let nature take its course. Ask for signs. Even if you don't know what is next, remember, that is still knowing something: what you don't want to have ever again! It is part of the honing process in life, deciding what is best, next. See #1.

I hope this list helps distract you in the best of ways possible.

Sometimes, we need to change the channel and tune in to something more uplifting.

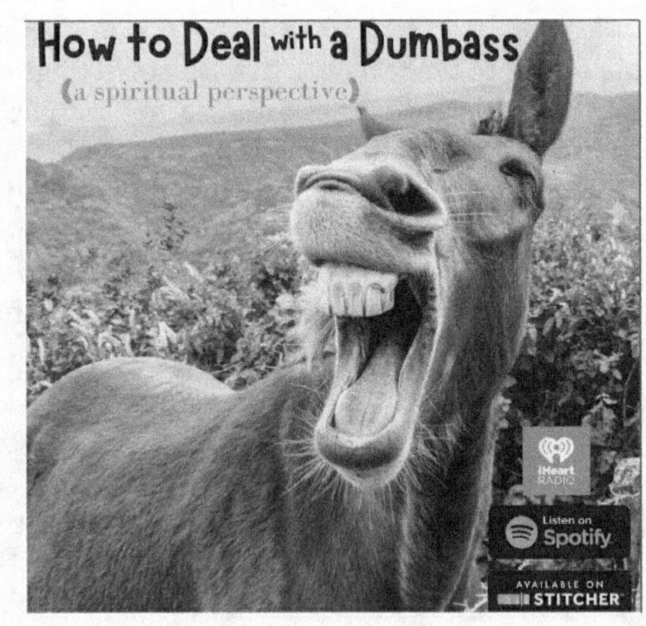

RESOURCES

This list was compiled to offer additional ways to cultivate support in your life.

Call 988 not 911 unless someone is hurt and in need of immediate assistance.

https://988lifeline.org/talk-to-someone-now/

There are many reasons besides suicidal thoughts that people can connect with the 988 Lifeline.

The 988 Lifeline responds 24/7 to calls, chats or texts from anyone who needs support for suicidal, mental health, and/or substance use crisis, and connects those in need with trained crisis counselors. Some examples in addition to thoughts of suicide are feeling overwhelmed with anxiety, sexual orientation worries, drinking too much, drug use, feeling depressed, mental and physical illness, loneliness, trauma, relationships, and economic worries.

Seeing someone else's story of recovery can help so much. It starts here: Moving America's Soul on Suicide | The Official Film

First responders and veterans can find a unique system and options for helping with PTSD. https://22zero.org

22Zero uses a peer-to-peer program for veterans, law enforcement, firefighters, 9-11 dispatchers, corrections, EMT/Paramedic, spouses, and minor children living in the home, and Gold Star Families, are covered at NO cost, to heal trauma.

Their mission is to heal and train veterans, first responders, and Gold Star Families using a non-invasive, non-clinical, peer-to-peer, holistic intervention, to save lives and families of our heroes, while ending suicide and trauma with the Trauma Resiliency Protocol and Emotions Management Process, across the U.S.

"Next Door" app - start a support group in your local area using this neighborhood app for connecting with others, like you, who know that reaching out, feeling heard, and not alone make a huge difference to one's mental health.

https://www.instagram.com/realdepressionproject/

https://thedepressionproject.com/products/this-is-how-you-overcome-depression-a-guided-treatment-plan

Suggestions from the professionals at 988 - When discussing suicide, especially on social media:
Report on suicide as a public health issue, not a crime.

Don't quote the suicide note or describe the method used.

Instead of describing the rate of recent suicides as an "epidemic," or "skyrocketing," carefully investigate the most recent Center for Disease Control data and use non-sensational words like "rise" or "higher."

Most people who die by suicide exhibit warning signs. Refrain from describing a suicide as "inexplicable" or "without warning."

Avoid quoting police or other first responders about causes of suicide. Instead, seek advice from suicide prevention experts, like the Lifeline.

Don't refer to suicide as "successful," "unsuccessful," or a "failed attempt." Use "died by suicide," "completed suicide," or "killed him/herself."

Develop policies and procedures for safe commenting and monitor for hurtful messages or comments from posters who may be in crisis. **Consider posting the Lifeline information in the first comment box in any story about suicide.**

On the global front, with politicians taking actions clearly not in the people's best interest, doing a real number on people's mental health, remember taking action alleviates anxiety.

There are actions we can take to create the change we want to see for ourselves and our children, instead of feeling like a 'sitting duck.'

For instance, elected officials can be removed from office, quickly, effectively, and with just nine signatures. This website will walk you through the steps to take action in your local community: https://bondsforthewin.com/# Their success stories include entire city councils being removed for failing to serve the public (a performance bond revocation) and mothers who'd had enough of masks being placed on their young children's faces.

When someone calls you for help, answer the phone and/or call them back when you say you will. It can be the difference between life or death.

RATTLED AWAKE

Over the last five years, what shook you up, and what did you do about it? How are you better, not bitter?

This chapter-book series is focused on pivots for the positive, as lived by "everyday" people with extraordinary stories to share.

Rattled Awake Volumes 1-11

This link will take you to the series, now 11 volumes strong.